Martina Naubert

Transactional Analysis Fairy World

Psychological fairy tales for adults
for inner growth

My dearest thanks to Annemieke and Paulus, who supported me
during this work with such valuable feed-back.

The stories

The 'Transactional Analysis Fairy World" is a collection of new fairy tales written for adults who consider their inner growth a never-ending process. The short stories are written in style and language of traditional fairy tales. Fairy tales have an unconscious impact on the reader or listener. That is why, even though these stories are based on the philosophy of Transactional Analysis, anybody can enjoy reading them without any knowledge on theory or models. The stories are self-contained without fixed sequence, taking place in the same kingdom with many characters featured throughout. The tales break open traditional role models without losing fascination of their historical ancestors.

The author

Martina Naubert is a trained Transactional Analysis facilitator (DGTA Germany). She has been working as Management Consultant and trainer for over 25 years. During this time, she held the position of Director of Human Resources, and later became CEO in a major corporation in Italy. During her many years of experience, she worked with people at all levels of employment, including top management. This allowed her to gain a great deal of experience in solving a wide range of problems at a very practical level. As a writer, Martina Naubert has drawn from the richness of her extensive background to create a number of adult fairy tales which can be used to either gain individual insight into one's personal growth or simply for one's reading pleasure. Either way, readers will be the richer for bringing these fairy tales into their lives. Martina Naubert was born in Vancouver, Canada, grew up in former West Germany and is now living with her family in Bologna, Italy. She continues to do in-depth work with Transactional Analysis.

Martina Naubert

Transactional

Analysis

Fairy World

Psychological fairy tales for adults
for inner growth

Transactional Analysis Fairy World

Printed and published by BoD –
Books on Demand, Norderstedt, Germania

ISBN: 9783752623475

Content

"We think fairy tales are for children. Nonsense!

As if we wanted to live in a world without fantasy at any age!"

Friedrich Wilhelm Nietzsche

(1844-1900)

The Secret Little Book

Once upon a time, in a kingdom far away, lived two millers. Each of them owned a beautiful mill. One was built at a clear creek in the south of the kingdom and the other at an equally refreshing little river in the north. Everybody in the kingdom knew them as the Miller of the North and the Miller of the South. Both were wealthy men, because they ground whole-wheat flour of an excellent quality. Even the cook of the royal castle purchased from them.

One day, it happened that a group of farmers, who all had their grain ground at the mill, came to see the Miller of the North. They asked his permission to take a little water from the creek in order to sprinkle their fields on hot summer days. The Miller thought about their request. He was worried that the big wheel of his mill might no longer turn strong enough in case they took too much water from the creek. The thought worried him. But he was afraid that if he refused their request, they would go to have their grain ground by the Miller of the South. So he did not say anything and agreed. He told himself that he could still discuss the matter if there was a problem in the future.

The miller had a secret little book where he noted everything he never spoke out. This little book was his hidden treasure. One day, he was certain, it would prove how good a man he had always been!

So he went ahead and noted all his worries. Soon he felt better and forgot all about it.

While the farmers were busily digging ditches, the cook of the royal castle stopped at the mill. He asked the miller to sell all his flour to him, because he had to prepare a big feast. The miller thought about his request. He needed a little stock of flour as all the bakeries in the kingdom of the north and south counted on him for running their business. If he sold all the flour to the Royal Cook he would have nothing left for the bakeries. However, because the Royal Cook was an important man of high influence, the miller did not say a word. He told himself that he could still discuss the matter later, if it should cause a problem. Until then, he would note all his worries in his little secret book. Soon he felt better and forgot all about it.

The next day the Royal Cook came back to load all bags of flour onto his carriage. Along with him was the youngest Princess who had never seen a mill before. Her mother had sent her to watch and learn about the life and the business of the people in the kingdom, so she could be a good Queen one day.

While the Royal Cook loaded the big bags onto his carriage, the Miller of the North showed the little Princess the big wheel that turned the heavy grinding stones to produce the flour. While listening and watching carefully, the little girl joyfully patted and cuddled the miller's cat.

When the Royal Cook had finished his work and was ready to drive back to the castle, the little Princess begged the miller to give her the cat as a present to remember the beautiful visit to his mill.

The miller thought about her request. Without a cat, all the mice who loved the grain in the mill, would surely take over. And a mice plague in a mill could be a very serious situation! But alas, it was the royals' little daughter who had asked him, and he did not dare to refuse. He let her have the cat. He told himself that he could still discuss the matter later, if the problem should grow out of hand. And once again he noted his worries in his little secret book. Soon he felt better and forgot all about it.

The days passed happily and the Miller of the North did not think of his notes in his secret little book anymore. Until one morning, he awoke and no longer heard the familiar turning sound of the cracking wooden wheel. He rushed outside to see what had caused this unusual silence.

It was a terrible shock!

The once clear creek had turned into a tiny little trickle and the big wheel stood totally still.

"Dear me! Dear me!", cried the Miller of the North tearing out his hair with great despair. "What misfortune! There is not enough water anymore to keep the mill working! Dear me! Dear me!"

He remembered the request of the farmers and he decided to go see them immediately and withdraw his permission to take water from his creek.

When the first farmer saw him approaching, he friendly waved his arm and shouted: "I say, you do come at the right moment! It saves me the travel! Surely you bring my flour for which I have given you my grain?!"

The Miller of the North remembered the Royal Cook to whom he had sold all the flour in stock, including that of the farmer.

"Dear me!", he cried to himself. "What can be done? All the flour is in the castle! Dear me!"

So he decided to drive to the castle and demand that a part of the flour should be returned.

Quickly he ran back to the mill in search of his little secret book, where all proof of his favour was noted. However, the moment he opened the door hundreds of mice rapidly scattered. They had built their nests in every corner of the mill and even all around the big wooden wheel that no longer turned.

"Dear me! Dear me!", cried the Miller of the North. "A mill with mice is the good miller's ruin! Dear me!"

He remembered the gift to the little Princess and decided to request back his cat. He would go to the castle immediately and take along the secret little book. At this point, only the King and the Queen themselves could help him out of his misery!

He saddled his horse and rode towards the castle, which was visible from far on a hill in the middle of the realm.

"Dear Queen and dearest King", whined the Miller of the North when he had arrived. "I am the most pitiful man in the kingdom! I have always been a good and upright person. I have given everybody what they wanted. This little book carries the proof of it! But, alas, nobody cares for my wellbeing! In return for my kindness they have ruined me!"

And he went on telling precisely how it had happened that his mill now was without water to turn the big wheel, that there was no flour left in stock and most of all, that he was punished with a plague of mice.

The Queen and the King listened carefully.

Finally, after long consideration, they came to a decision.

"Dear Miller of the North, we cannot help you in this matter", the King spoke. "There is no law on how much water you have to leave to the farmers. There is no law on how much flour you have to

11

sell. And there is no law that obliges you to give away your cat - not even to a Princess. You have to solve this matter yourself."

"That's not fair!", cried the Miller of the North.

He did not want to accept that he had created his fate himself. He stomped away furiously, out through the big castle's gate. With each step he became more aggravated, as he knew deep inside that the King and the Queen were right.

And the farther he went on, the more his grudge grew into an outrageous inner fire.

Full of irrepressible fury he was about to burst and turned - puff - into an evil dragon. Driven by sheer anger he swallowed every single page of the secret little book without even chewing and stomped towards the forest, spitting fire each step of his way.

At the same time, some farmers spoke to the Miller of the South as well.

They also asked to be allowed to draw water from the little river for their ditches. Like the Miller of the North before, the Miller of the South also thought that he needed the water to turn the big wheel. And he also did not want to upset the peasants, because they had been good customers to him for many years. So he answered:

"If you want to dig the water behind my mill, that shall be fine with me! Once the water has turned the wheel, you can use it for your fields."

A little later the castle's master chef came to buy all his flour supplies for an excellent feast in the castle. But the Miller of the South replied:

"I can only give you two-thirds of my supply. I need the rest to carry on my business."

The Royal Cook became angry with him and pointed out that the flour was for the royal court. He threatened to tell the Queen and the king.

But the Miller of the South suggested with all his courage:

"If you buy some potatoes and chestnuts from the farmers, I can prepare flour of a different kind for you. It's not as fine as whole wheat flour. But you can create new dishes, which will be a wonderful surprise for your guests!"

The idea appealed to the master chef and he agreed.

When he later that week brought the potatoes and chestnuts into the mill, the youngest Prince jumped off the wagon. His sister had told him about the mill, where she had been given the beautiful cat. He also wanted to see a mill and take a cat as a gift.

The Miller of the South feared as well that the King would be angry with him if he did not comply with this request. Already, and only with the utmost courage and wisdom, had he persuaded the master chef to buy some different flour. Therefore, he was not comfortable when he answered the little Prince:

"I cannot give you my cat. I need it to catch mice and keep the mill clean."

Angrily the little Prince crossed his arms in front of his chest.

"The Miller of the North gave my sister a cat!", he huffed.

The master chef also looked grimly at the Miller of the South.

"Well", the miller replied wisely, "perhaps the Miller of the North had two cats and could therefore give one away? However, I only have this one. I may give it to you, but only after the last mouse is trapped. If you want to wait until then, we shall agree?"

The little Prince thought about it. The offer seemed fair to him and after a while he nodded in agreement.

He did not continue to insist on his wish and rode back with the cook to the castle.

As the Miller of the North was no longer seen, from that day on, all the farmers carried their grain to the Miller of the South. His cat continued to catch mice and since she was well nourished and healthy, next spring she gave birth to six little kittens in a corner of the mill. The Miller of the South chose the smallest among them and brought it to the castle to the little Prince, redeeming his promise earlier than he had anticipated.

Soon the Miller of the South had to expand his mill and hire apprentices because he could not manage to do all the work by himself anymore. He also mounted blades on the roof of his mill so that he could use both, water and wind, to grind grain. His mill grew into a big and flourishing business and became famous throughout the kingdom and beyond.

But since that day, a wicked dragon was feared in the deep forest, bringing dread and fright to anyone who would venture to go there.

The Embroidered Coat

One day, a tailor and a seamstress made their entrance in a small town far away, where way up, on top of the hill, there was a royal castle with a King and a Queen.

The tailor and the seamstress were dressed in strange long garments and the woman wore a red dot in the middle of her forehead. People had never seen anything like it before, which caused them to interrupt their activities and turn their heads as they walked by.

The strange couple bought a house at the end of the road and put up a large sign. From that day on everybody could read in large letters: "TAILORING".

Soon they got settled and not long after a little baby girl was born.

The two tailors were very nimble with needle and thread and exceedingly skillful with the fabrics they had brought along from a foreign country. Soon many people started to have their garments for special occasions tailored by them and their business was thriving.

The daughter grew up into a pretty young girl and learned the craft from her parents. She wore, like her mother, a red dot on her forehead and by that time the people in the kingdom did not find it strange anymore.

They could have been the happiest family in the whole kingdom, if it had not been for little vicious habits that had taken over their routine in all these years.

In the morning the seamstress got up and started a fire, so it would be cozy and warm in the room. Her husband would eat a piece of bread, drink a cup of warm milk and then go to work well-nourished and with renewed energy. He pulled his nightcap off his head, threw it carelessly on the kitchen table and started working. Thus, every morning he began his day cheerfully whistling, for he was well rested and always in a good mood.

His wife, however, gave a loud sigh every time she saw her husband being careless and because he did not want to spoil his good mood, he whistled all the louder.

Ever since they had come to this distant kingdom, this had become their morning routine.

At noon, the woman sent her daughter to the bakery to buy fresh bread for the meal. At that hour, it was the tailor's task to fetch firewood for the stove so his wife could cook the meal.

"I'll do it right away", he always said, "I'm just going to finish this one seam!"

And so he plunged his head back into his work until the daughter came home again. Since the girl did not want her parents to quarrel about the firewood, she ran out right away and brought an arm full of wood into the kitchen. But as much as she tried, every time her dress got dirty and her mother gave another deep sigh.

Ever since they had come to this distant kingdom, this had become their routine every noon.

In the evening the man finally put aside his work, rubbed his eyes and stretched himself. Then he stood up from his place and stepped outside for a little walk in front of the house. And again, his wife gave a deep sigh, even louder than the one in the morning and the one at noon. He always heard it, but since she never spoke, he did not see any need to turn around and talk to her about it. Instead, he would quickly go outside.

Eventually, his wife would rise from her work, and gather the fabric remnants, which he always left scattered on the table. She sighed again and began to fold them before storing them away into the chests used for this purpose.

Ever since they had come to this distant kingdom, this had become their evening routine.

It had been like this for a long time, day after day, month after month, year after year and the tailor and his daughter had gotten used to the fact that the seamstress would spend many hours sighing. Until one day, however, when she had run out of alleviating sighs.

The wife had begun to make a new winter cloak for her husband, so he would be able to deliver their creations to customers far away, even in the cold season. Whenever she had had a little spare time, she had work on it.

That day, she took the almost finished coat in her hands and began to embroider it in fine letters:

Nightcap in the bed box!
Fabric remnants in the chest!

And in particularly large letters she embroidered:
FIRE WOOD!!!!

In order for the words to be legible, she had the blacksmith forge a metal thread, similar to those used for the royal knight's chain armor.

She worked for many days at the new embroidery. This was a laborious task, but she found her work thoroughly satisfactory and it made her feel very good about herself. From then on, no more sighs escaped her chest.

Her husband was in the best of moods because his wife had ceased to sigh before the day began. The daughter was pleased because her mother no longer moaned when she dirtied her dress and in the evening the tailor was relieved when he went for walks without hearing his wife sighing. Now, all three of them actually believed that they were the happiest people in the whole kingdom.

Until one day, when the first snow fell, the tailor had to go out to deliver a new dress to the wife of the administrator at the royal castle. The lady dressmaker prepared the package for delivery. She handed it over to her husband and said:

"It has become cold. Take this new coat here, which I have tailored for you for the winter. I put a lot of effort in the embroidery. You may read my stitching carefully as you are on your way. "

And thus, she closed the door behind her husband and went back to work. She busied herself for many hours, more carefree and happier than she had been for a long time.

She eagerly awaited her husband's return.

But he did not come back home.

It became dark and a cold wind started whistling around the house. A heavy snowstorm came down and the blizzard was so bad that one could hardly see the other houses on the opposite side of the road.

At that sight the lady dressmaker became afraid and she said to her daughter:

"Your father is not yet back. Maybe he cannot find the way with all the snow? We have to go look for him!"

The girl wrapped herself in a blanket and hurried out to her friends. She managed to get the son of the blacksmith and the two brothers of the mayor to ride off with their horses to search for the tailor.

Soon they found him sitting rigidly in a pile of snow at the roadside, in front of the town gate.

The young lads tried to pull him onto one of the horses, but the man's cloak was so heavy that they could not lift him. So they called more friends for help. Only when there were six lads did they succeed in hoisting the tailor onto a handcart and drag him home.

There they put him on a chair in front of the fire, so that the snow, which covered him from head to toe, would melt.

"Take off the coat. It's warm in here, you don't need it here anymore!", said the daughter and wanted to remove the garment from him.

But she could not strip off the coat.

The lady dressmaker and the girl pulled both with all their might, each at one sleeve, but neither the cloak nor the tailor moved an inch.

"It is not possible," wailed the tailor. "I cannot move."

The seamstress and her daughter stood in front of the father not knowing what to do. He seemed tied to the chair by his cloak.

"The coat surely is frozen and it is so stiff that you cannot take if off!", the daughter spoke to her father. "If you stay here in front of the fire, the ice will melt eventually and it will be soft enough tomorrow morning!"

According to this plan they put more firewood into the oven and lay down to sleep.

The next morning the tailor sat as they had left him, motionless and stiff in his cloak. This time he did not whistle, because he had slept poorly and was in a bad mood. His daughter brought him a piece of bread and a cup of warm milk, but he continued to show a grim face.

Then the seamstress took the big fabric scissors and said:

"It hurts me in my soul to cut this coat, but it has to be done!"

However, as much as she tried, she did not succeed in getting the scissors to cut into the thick fabric. She could not even separate the seams.

The seamstress and her daughter paced around the chair, rubbing their chins while thinking hard. The mother took a right turn, the daughter a left. What could be done?

The tailor looked from one to the other, until he got dizzy and finally said:

"It's no use running in circles! Go to the blacksmith and ask him to come with his iron tongs! "

But even the blacksmith could not do anything with the big pliers. The cloak kept the tailor stiff and firmly trapped.

By now, good advice was more than precious!

At that point the seamstress gathered all her courage, wrapped her warm shoulder stole tightly, and walked to the front door: "I will go to the royal castle and ask the Queen herself for advice."

It took a whole day trudging through heavy snow until she finally reached the royal palace. All the while she had lived in the town, she had seen it only from afar on the hill in the middle of the kingdom and she marveled, because it was much more magnificent and splendid than she had imagined.

The Queen listened to her in silence for a long time as the seamstress related to her the whole story of the mishap with her husband's cloak. Even when she had finished and remained in anxious silence, the Queen said nothing and just looked at the lady dressmaker for a long time.

"Well", she said, finally breaking the silence, "There is only one thing you can do."

She reached into a fruit bowl, which stood beside the throne on a table, handed the woman a fruit and said:

"Feed this apple to your husband. It's for every sigh you have given in the morning! "

The woman reached for the apple and nodded.

"Feed this prune to your husband. It's for every sigh you have given at noon."

The lady dressmaker took the dried plum.

"And feed him especially this nut. It's for every sigh you have given in the evening."

The lady dressmaker also took the nut and kept the fruits in the pockets of her skirt. She thanked the Queen and was about to leave.

"Take this lantern too, so that you can find the way in the darkness," the Queen added.

That was very wise, because it was a moonless night, so dark that the woman would have probably lost her way. The light of the lantern, however, led her in the right direction and as the sun rose, she arrived at the town gate and hurried towards her home.

She did as advised by the Queen and when the tailor had eaten the apple, which she had shoved into his mouth little by little, the threads of her first embroidery slowly started dissolving. The seamstress quickly pulled the yarn out of the woolen cloak. And when she did, the heavy thread of iron turned into a shining twist of pure silver.

Overjoyed by this success she immediately fed her husband the dried plum. And again, the embroidery softened and this time, the thread turned into a golden ribbon.

Even more encouraged by this accomplishment, she also wanted to feed him the nut. But the tailor was full and wanted nothing more to eat. He shook his head and pressed his lips together.

He tried to move, but the coat still held him prisoner. Finally, he gave a deep sigh and agreed to also eat the nut.

The remaining embroideries came apart and the woman pulled out a never-ending fine diamond thread.

When the last thread was pulled, the tailor jumped on his legs and hopped joyfully around the room, even though he still wore the warm coat. He grabbed his wife by her shoulders and whirled her dancing through the parlor. They spent the whole day in happiness, dancing and singing and singing and dancing.

The next day they started weaving the precious threads from the cloak into the most beautiful fabrics, of which they made magnificent garments.

From that day on, even the Queen had her dresses made by the tailors couple, because nowhere in the whole country did one find such magnificent fabrics.

The tailor shop's reputation became well known in and far beyond the kingdom. The daughter learned the art of valuable yarn spinning, ensuring a well-deserved income for the rest of their lives.

And, until the end of their days, no more sighs were ever heard in the house of the tailors.

The Lord of the Knights

Once upon a time, long ago, in a kingdom far away, with a magnificent castle on top of a mountain right in the centre of the kingdom, every year a knights' tournament was held for the Queen's birthday.

Numerous noble horsemen from many countries came to compete. Each one of them aimed to bring home the Trophy of Victory to his own kingdom.

Over the years the tournament had become such a great success that every year more horsemen came.

After some time the knights of the kingdom began to grumble, because it happened more and more often that a stranger won the precious trophy and all the spectators cheered only for this foreign winner.

"That's not right," they said to the castle's administrator, whose job it was to organize the competitions. "We are the knights of this kingdom. People do not even know when they cheer for strangers, because all of them wear armors like we do. They cannot be distinguished from us!"

In order to suppress the resentment of the knights, the good man promised to consider their concern. He was very well aware, however, that it was the royal couple, who invited the guests from afar, not him! And he would risk falling into disgrace, if he let the tournament take place without the guests.

He had many sleepless nights, turning and twisting in his bed, thinking about what could be done to appease the knights, and at the same time, not to aggravate the King and the Queen.

But no good idea would come to his mind. It seemed quite an impossible task to him.

After a few days of futile reflection, he decided to take the road down to the town's tavern to discuss the matter with his friends. Maybe they would have an idea?

He knew his way very well, because he walked it once a week. It had been his habit for a long time, the last day of the week, always at the same hour, to share a mug of beer with the Blacksmith, the

Tailor and the Seamstress and the Miller of the South. They were good enough friends and he surely could ask them for advice.

So, he went on his way, his head bent down in thought.

But this time, when he arrived at the foot of the hill of the castle, where the road turns towards the town, nothing seemed as usual.

Where normally only field flowers surrounded an old oak tree, now there was a wooden wagon with a white horse. In front of the carriage sat an old man, propped leaning on a stick.

"Well, well!", the timeworn old man spoke. "What happened to you, good fellow? Is something troubling you to make such a grim face?"

The castle's administrator stopped and shrugged his shoulders.

"Each one has his own sorrows", he answered and wanted to carry on.

But the old man blocked his way with his cane.

"For that, I am just the right person!", he claimed and pointed with his stick to a colorful sign with large letters on the wagon.

"Wonder Maker", he read aloud.

"I do not need a miracle, but some good advice may not hurt", said the castle administrator.

"I have helped many a desperate! Just tell me what your troubles are."

Subsequently, the castle's administrator told the old man of his predicament and that, no matter what he would decide, either the knights or the royal couple would be upset with him.

"But nothing's easier than that!", uttered the old man, beckoning him to come closer.

When the good man was near enough, he drew him closer and whispered in his ear:

"There shall be two trophies: One for the knights of this kingdom and one for the strangers!"

"That is indeed some good advice!", rejoiced the administrator. "You know your business well!"

"Just beware and tell no one that you have this suggestion from me!", added the old man. "It will not be an advantage, if people think that such a good idea could not come from yourself!"

The administrator nodded eagerly, paid with a silver coin and carried on. He felt more than relieved.

But the castle's administrator did not know that the old man was a disguised wicked wizard, who lived on the top of a high mountain in a forlorn ancient house behind the forest. He had heard of the resentment of the knights and recognized the long-awaited opportunity for him, to finally seize the power in the kingdom. He had always wanted to live in the magnificent castle on the hill himself. And now, this naive castle's administrator was so easy to influence! He simply had to pursue his plan until he would be the lord of the knights and the King of the whole realm.

The wanderer barely was out of sight, when the wizard jumped on his horse and rode off into the night, laughing aloud.

The following year it came as a surprise to everybody, that there were two winners. But people cheered for both alike. The tournament was an even bigger success than ever and the guests from the other kingdoms congratulated the royal couple for such a great event.

The new idea appealed that much to the Queen that she spoke:

"Next year we will even invite all the courageous girls of the kingdoms to this tournament. Those women, who wish to compete with knights, are also welcome to participate. It is going to be an exciting tournament!"

The lady messenger of the castle, who was famous for being faster than any other messenger, heard the communication with great joy. She was an experienced rider and wanted to compete with the knights. From that moment on, every evening, she practiced diligently in armor. She became soon familiar with it and very capable in handling the knights' weapons.

The year after, it was yet another surprise to everybody that one of the two winners actually turned out to be the lady messenger. She was overjoyed and especially the Queen congratulated her dearly on her success. And when all the other women witnessed that a girl had a fair chance to win, many of them wanted to take part in the competition the following year.

The wicked wizard, nonetheless, had not stayed away from the tournament. He had mingled with the knights, hidden in black armor. While the lady messenger received her trophy from the Queen and the king, he maliciously whispered to the knights:

"It is quite difficult for us that a woman should participate in the tournament in such an open way. No real noble knight will ever fight a lady! He will always give precedence to her, as it is the rule of honour for every true knight!"

"That is indeed correct!", cried the knights. "It is a rather unequal battle! As genuine knights we can never win!"

They hurried to the castle's administrator to report to him their annoyance.

"That is not right," they said. "We are the noble knights of this kingdom and must honour women, as it has always been the rule for true knights. How can we ever win such a contest?"

To appease the resentment of the knights, the administrator promised to think about it.

This time he immediately took off to the old oak tree.

Sure enough, he found the carriage with the white horse and the old man in front of it. His relief was so great that he handed the old man a silver coin before he had even spoken.

"I need your advice again!", he hurried to say. And he reported, how it had happened that he found himself again in the same miserable situation as a year earlier.

"Nothing easier than that!", replied the old man, beckoning the wanderer to come closer so he could whisper in his ear:

"It is the hair of the ladies that distracts the knights. Therefore, they shall never open the visor. That way, a knight will not know, if he competes against a man or a woman."

"That is indeed some good advice!", replied the administrator. "You know your business well!"

The castle's administrator thanked the wizard and wanted to go hastily on his way. But the evil magician held him back.

"I hear, that this year not a single noble knight of our kingdom has won a trophy?"

The administrator moaned a little and stepped unsteadily from one foot to the other. In fact, he had already worried that the knights would soon come to him with this complaint.

"That is right," he admitted. "But the girl and the stranger have won in an honest manor and I cannot do anything about it."

The old man seized his cane and swayed it with anger in the air.

"People speak unwell about it! It displeases them that a stranger and a girl defeat the noble knights! The whole kingdom will be ashamed, if the noble knights are being embarrassed."

"Is it truly that, what people say?", asked the castle's administrator frightened, for he now thought that his situation was much more tragic than he had believed. If the tournament ceased to bring fame and glory to the Queen and King and the whole kingdom, he would be ruined.

He had been distressed before, but now he was desperate.

"If you want to hear me out, I should even have some excellent advice for you on that difficult matter", the magician proposed. "But it will cost more than one silver coin."

As the first two counsels had been such good ones, the castle's administrator was willing to pay any price for another one. He pulled two silver coins out of his purse, but the old man shook his head.

"Give me your word of honour that you will remain the faithful servant of the owner of the castle, for your entire life!"

The poor castle's administrator had always been loyal to the royal couple and considered the demanded payment easy to fulfill. He thought by himself, that this old man, who knew his business so well, was also very much attached to the royal family.

"I promise," he said solemnly without hesitation.

"Well," spoke the miracle maker. "Three things you have to do. First, make sure the ladies not only keep the visor closed, but also the helmet, day and night. Whoever will not follow this rule, will be excluded from the tournament forever."

The administrator nodded.

"Second, see to it that all strangers will always wear a red belt over their chest. That is easy to be done. Whoever will not follow this rule, will be excluded from the tournament forever."

Again, the administrator nodded.

"Third and last point, make it known to all the people in the kingdom, that they will be invited to a great feast at the castle, with music and dancing, free beer and food for everybody, but of course, only, if one of your own knights will win."

Since the first recommendations of the old man had been such good ones, the administrator accepted the three rules without thinking twice and considered them as another excellent solution to this difficulty.

"That I will do!", he spoke. "You know your business well!"

"Indeed, indeed!", mumbled the magician to himself, as the good man turned around and went on his way back towards the castle.

Soon the new regulations were communicated all over the kingdom. People in the empire were excited about the possibility of a great celebration in the castle they had never seen from the inside. They cheered and praised the royal couple for such generosity, never witnessed in any other kingdom before.

Everything was organized accordingly.

Because until that day, law and order had always been for their benefit, people did not question the new regulations and followed the instructions without hesitation.

A couple of days before the next tournament, when the first foreigner appeared with a red belt over his chest, people began observing him with suspicion. And they started to think that he or the other foreign knights should certainly not win the contest, if they wanted to have their royal buffet in the castle.

Meanwhile, the girls planning to participate, tried in vain to get some night's rest, in spite of the helmet they had to wear even in bed. They could not sleep anymore. After only one week many of them were so tired, they could not resist any longer. They took off the helmet. Every night, another one of them gave up.

Only the lady messenger persisted, even though she as well, was already so sleepy that she hardly could hold herself in the saddle, when she had to fulfill her duty of bringing messages across the country. However, she endured.

Finally, the great day arrived.

More spectators than ever went to the castle to watch the event. Nobody wanted to be left out from the promised royal celebration with free drink and food. Everybody wanted to be first to cheer on one of the kingdom's knights. The tribune was crowded with people and those, who were not lucky enough to have a seat, stood shoulder to shoulder tight around the tournament's area.

As the knights of the kingdom entered the arena, people applauded them with great excitement, enthusiastically waving flags of only their own kingdom. The wicked wizard rode in his black armor right amongst them. Nobody noticed him, because – as it was the new rule - they all kept their visor closed.

When finally, at last, the knights with the red belts entered the arena, people started booing them and whistled ferociously. Sure enough, one of them should not win the game! They definitely wanted to have their promised feast!

The Queen and the King watched in earnestness, because such a behavior had never been observed in the kingdom before. They could not understand why, all of a sudden, the people of their kingdom acted in such a hostile way.

As soon as the first competition began and a knight with a red belt made a skillful move, people shouted even louder and booed and hollered even more mercilessly. No matter how clever one of them rode, no matter how proficient one of them fought, only the knights of their own kingdom received cheers and applause from the crowd.

The royal couple sat silently, in great astonishment.

Then a knight in black armor appeared in the arena. With one stroke he kicked the other rider off his horse, before that one even had had a chance to bow before the King and the Queen, as courtesy requested. In spite of this unfair move, people howled in exaltation. And when the fallen horseman did not rise again, they stared dumbfounded with amazement.

The royal jester ran onto the field and tried to open the visor of the fallen knight to give him some water to drink, as it was his duty. But he could not open it, because its junctures were all corroded.

So, he pulled off the helmet and when long, shiny hair poured out of it, everybody could see that is was the lady messenger.

Thanks to the fresh water she had been offered, she opened her eyes, but because now, everybody had seen the young woman, instead of jumping back on horseback, she sadly had to leave the arena.

The black knight, with his head held high, galloped on his horse around in circles and gesticulated to the people to cheer him on again. And not for long, they screamed in such jubilation that nobody could hear any spoken word anymore.

At that sight, the Queen rose from her throne.

The black knight did not even look at her.

Instead, sure of himself and his next winning stroke, he led his horse in anticipation around the arena. Again and again, round and around he went, until he was surrounded by a wave of excitement.

At that very moment, a hush descended over the noisy crowd.

All heads turned towards the entrance where the Queen herself appeared on her black centaur. Her long white hair was flowing over her shoulders and she wore a red belt over her chest. Thus, she led her horse right in front of the black knight in the centre of the arena and made a clear sign with her hand that she desired to compete with him.

And as she stood there with her head up high, speaking not a single word, and not moving back an inch, people bowed their heads in shame.

Nobody dared to boo or whistle anymore.

Nobody dared to cheer either.

There was such complete silence that even a dropped needle would have made enough noise to scare the horses.

The wicked magician looked around and started swinging his pennant, in order to stir up emotions again and make everybody howl as before.

But instead of giving in to his attempts, this time people stepped back in silence, until the black knight stood isolated and alone in the centre of the arena.

The King rose from his throne and started slowly clapping his hands.

The royal jester followed his example and soon also the Princesses and Princes applauded in great respect. Gradually also the other people rose from their seats and joined the ovation.

But the black knight would not give up so easily.

He grabbed his lance in attack against the Queen in front of him.

At that very moment, all the knights of the kingdom stepped forward and stood by the side of their Queen.

Even the knights with their red belts took place next to their former competitors. The girls loosened their hair to let it flow in the wind and also started clapping their hands in this steady rhythm.

The black knight's horse began to become nervous and started bolting nervously, not knowing where to go. The evil wizard beat the poor animal in a fury, but the more he tried to spur it on, the wilder the creature became.

He tightened the reins, but instead of obeying his orders, the beast reared up, neighing in panic. Right there, all of a sudden, the animal's horseshoes flashed up in a color so red, just like a glowing fire and everyone recognized the evil rider for who he truly was.

In a blind fury the black knight tore off his helmet and showed his dark true face to everybody.

"I will come back!", he thundered and swung the spear through the air. "And then, there will be no escape! For none of you!"

However, by then everybody had joined in the clapping rhythm and people only stepped back to make way for the black knight to ride off.

But, again, he did not.

He spurred his horse and under the disbelieving gaze of all, the animal rose into the air, blasting with the evil wizard on its back, over the castle's buildings, into the breaking night, obscuring the sky for hours with thick clouds.

Nobody uttered a word.

No one could believe what they had just witnessed.

And yet, no one doubted that it really had happened.

"Go home!", the Queen said quietly. "Everybody go home!"

That evening, people sat in silence around the tables in the taverns or in their homes, and the guests quietly went back to their homelands.

For a long time, people in every country were speaking of this event and the courage demonstrated by the Queen with long white hair.

Red belts, however, were never seen again and it became an unspoken rule not to wear one.

The Golden Glasses

Once upon a time, in a small town in a kingdom far away lived three baker couples.

One couple were breadbakers and made fresh and healthy whole wheat loafs. The second couple specialized in baking cakes and they were famous for their excellent tarts and delicious pies. The third couple created the finest pralines and chocolates. They had come from a foreign country and had a dark skin, just like the chocolate they sold.

Each one of them ran a little shop right next to one of the big town gates that every person, who wanted to enter the old city, had to pass. Everybody in the kingdom went to this town, when they were in need of bread, cake or – for very special occasions – chocolate. Even the King and the Queen sent their servants to purchase at these bakeries.

The three couples had a good income and lived well and happily, going about their business peacefully and their customers were satisfied with their products.

But one day everything changed.

An old woman came to shop at the bread bakery.

She had a long way to walk from her tiny house outside the town, located along the way to the castle on top of the hill. As she put the loaf she had bought into her basket, she moaned:

"If only I didn't have to walk so far with my old legs to the other end of town, just to buy cake. Tomorrow my sister will come for a visit from another kingdom and I want to offer her some fine cakes. I am already tired, but now I still have to walk across town to the other gate to shop at the cake bakery. And that's not all! I will have to carry all my purchases the very long way back to my house. If only it would not be so far and tiresome!"

When the old woman had left the bakery, the lady baker thought about her words for a long time.

Suddenly she had an excellent idea.

At night she spoke to her husband:

"If we didn't only make bread, but also cakes, people would not have to walk so far to get both. They could buy it here in our shop. We could learn to bake cakes; don't you think so?"

Her husband liked the idea.

They didn't mince a lot of words before it was done.

A week later they presented a variety of cakes in the big window of their bakery in addition to their traditional products. Many of their customers were delighted and also bought, along with the loaf, a piece of cake.

"What an excellent idea!" everybody said, and they quickly passed on the news to their neighbours.

But, alas, as fate would have it, the wife of the chocolate baker passed by and discovered the large crowd of people in front of the bread bakery. When she understood the reason for this gathering, she hurried back to her husband to report what she had seen.

When he heard the news, he made a grim face, because he was afraid that the bread baker's couple could also come up with the idea of making chocolates. They quickly closed their shop and hurried to the cake makers' bakery.

Already from afar they could see the cake bakers couple in their store, looking with puzzled expressions on their faces at their unsold pastries in the window and wondering, why only so few people had bought anything today.

"Maybe the quality of the flour isn't good anymore?", the man said to his wife. "Tomorrow I will speak to the Miller of the South about it!"

When they saw the chocolate bakers couple enter their shop at this time of day, the cake bakers speculated even more. At this hour they should be busy selling their pralines and chocolates, instead of wandering leisurely through town?

"It certainly is none of our business", spoke the chocolate baker to the cake bakers couple. "But we will strongly support you, no matter what!! You must know, it is the bread baker's fault that nobody buys your cake anymore. My wife has seen it with her own eyes."

So that was the reason for this unfortunate development!

The cake bakers couple sighed deeply.

It was the fault of the bread bakers! How in the world could they have had such an evil idea? Why would they make their lives so miserable? They had never done them any harm!

The chocolate baker rubbed his chin in disgust.

Instead of groaning, like the cake bakers couple did, they decided that something had to be done about this problem!

"Tomorrow we will go to the bread baker's store!", he suggested. "We will put up a sales stand right in front of their shop. And not only will we sell cake and chocolates, but also bread. And, for a better price! Surely they will understand that message!"

That is how it came to be that early next morning, when the bread bakers opened their window shutters, they found many people gathering in front of their shop.

"Fresh bread!", yelled the wife of the cake baker behind a counter, loaded with bread loafs and cakes. Next to her there was another table, where the chocolate lady baker shouted: "Fresh buns, still crispy and warm, right out of the oven!"

Their husbands were so busy packing up all the bread and buns they sold, that they did not even notice the bread baker, who came running out of the house. He and his wife were still wearing their aprons and were covered from head to toe with flour from their early morning work of rolling out dough.

Thus they rushed out to the stands and pushed aside the customers surrounding them.

"What gives you the right to come here in front of our store to sell bread!?", the bread baker screamed wildly and clapped his hands full of flour right into the face of the lady cake baker.

The poor woman stood in amazement, her face white like a ghost. Only her eyes blinked like two black holes and she had to sneeze.

"It was you who started the problem! I am certain it must have been the idea of your greedy wife to offer not only bread, but also cake!?", the wife of the chocolate baker argued ferociously in defense of her friend next to her. She plunged her hands into the chocolate powder and clapped them right into the face of the bread baker's wife.

The poor woman stood perplexed; her face completely brown like a bear. Only her eyes blinked like two white holes as she sneezed.

At that the bread baker grabbed a pie from the stand and answered the chocolate lady baker: "How dare you attack my wife?!"

"Put back my pie immediately, will you!", the cake baker screamed in his turn, trying to pry the pie from the other person's hands.

But he lost his balance and fell with his face right into the sweet creamy pastry that the bread baker was fiercely holding on to.

The people around them had stepped aside, in order to watch with great amusement, but from a safe distance. Everybody laughed with glee, when the cake baker stood covered with cream all over his face, and the two women all white and brown at his side.

This was so entertaining! They laughed so hard tears streamed down their faces, and some had to hold their tummies, shaking with laughter.

"You dare!", the chocolate baker shrieked, grabbing a praline and rubbing it on the nose of the bread baker.

It didn't take long before a grand battle had started. Bread, cake and chocolate flew through the air. Soon the fighting parties had cream in their hair, flour and chocolate powder in their faces, cake all over and pastry on their backs. Even sticky dough was flung at their heads.

Children took advantage of the opportunity and grabbed a few sweets, because they thought it was too sad to see all these goodies go to waste. People from all over town rushed by to witness the spectacle. They had not had such fun and good laughter in a very long time! And besides, never had they picked up secretly so many delicious bits and pieces without paying.

Only when there was nothing left to throw, the fighting parties eventually stopped. The bread baker and his wife stomped back into their house and slammed the window shutters in anger. The cake and chocolate baker couples gathered their remaining goodies and went away. As there was nothing left to see or eat, the spectators dispersed and went home as well.

The next day none of the bakers opened their shop, because they had nothing left to sell and their bones hurt so much, that they were unable to get back to work.

The cake bakers blamed the chocolate bakers to have gotten them involved into this unfortunate fight. The bread bakers were angry with the cake bakers, because they had only wanted to offer their customers a shorter way for shopping. They felt they were being treated in an unfair way. On the other hand, the chocolate bakers felt hurt, since they had only wanted to help their friends.

All of them were so busy blaming the others for this very unfortunate situation that they forgot all about their business. Soon there was no more bread around and people had nothing left to eat along with their meals. Not to mention any sweets. The Miller of the South had to send his workers home, because the bakeries no longer bought flour. And since the Miller bought no more grain from the farmers, they too, lost their income.

Eventually misery came over the whole kingdom.

That serious situation was anything but amusing and people started wishing that the fight would never have taken place.

But nobody knew how to solve the problem now!

The bakers kept their shutters closed and locked themselves up in their shops, pouting and blaming the others.

When finally, the Queen and the King heard about the affair, because even in the castle there was not one loaf of bread left, they sent out their eldest children to check what was going on. The Princess and the Prince drove to town in their coach and talked to each of the three baker couples. But each of them insisted they were right and demanded understanding from the others. There was nothing the Princess and Prince could do to make any of them change their mind.

So, they made their way back to the castle to report to their parents.

When they passed the little house at the bottom of the hill, where the old woman lived, the woman brought the coach to a stop and handed a small wooden box to the young royals inside.

"Give these Golden Glasses to the person who can see through them!"

Being curious, the Prince took the glasses out of the box and put them on his nose. But he could not see anything. In vain his sister tried to do better, but neither she could see.

"The only one who can see through these glasses, will be the person who knows the truth!", the old woman said. "Go and find this person!"

So the Prince and Princess turned around and called the three bakers couples into the town hall. Without explaining a word they demanded one after the other to try on the Golden Glasses.

With great reluctance the three baker men finally did so, with much grumbling. But the glasses were useless to them.

"Now it's the bakers' wives turn to try these glasses on!", the Prince said handing them over to the bread baker's wife to go first.

When she took the Golden Glasses, she remembered the old woman and said: "These are the glasses of the old woman who had come to our shop! She had complained deeply about the tiresome long way she had to come."

And as she put on the glasses, all of a sudden, she could see clearly.

She spoke to her fellow bakers:

"Each one of us felt treated unfairly. Each one of us thought to be right. But actually, none of us was! We were all wrong, each in our way. There cannot be a winner in this drama, each one of us can only lose. So, listen to me, here is what we can do. You, cake bakers, shall make cake! You know best how to do this. And you two, chocolate bakers, make sweets and pralines! You know best how to do that. And we make bread, because it is, what we know best. But from now on, we all shall offer to our customers each other's' products!"

She handed the glasses over to the cake baker.

He put them on again, and this time, he also could see clearly.

"Indeed!", he said, "that way people do not have to walk far, because they will find whatever they need in every bakery shop!"

He presented the glasses to the chocolate baker and he, too, could see all of a sudden.

"Yes!", he cried out. "This way we share our work and all our products will always be of top quality!"

Now the bread baker, too, wanted to test the glasses and put them on. And one after the other who tested the glasses, saw and agreed.

And so, from that day on, all bakery shops in town offered the goods of the other bakeries. Customers went shopping where it was most convenient to them and everybody was satisfied.

Soon the butchers discussed the idea and cooperated in the same way. Then the vegetable farmers did, the pot makers and the weavers and the dressmakers. The town became wealthy and many travelers came from far to look at and buy from the variety of goods offered in this town.

The Golden Glasses, however, were carefully kept in a showcase in the town hall. Every citizen in need of settling a fight was allowed to use them, although nobody was allowed to take them home.

So, often someone could be found sitting in silence for a long time in the town hall, hoping to finally see.

And, yes, sometimes it happened, that this someone actually understood.

The Two Snake Charmers

Once, in a kingdom far, far away, where the King was called Sultan and Governor Pasha there lived a powerful Emperor. He was a proficient and strong ruler. His people lived well, because he was good at encouraging trade and craftsmanship, and able to unite all the knights of his kingdom.

All over the empire splendid buildings and superb castles, with walls decorated with ornaments of gold and precious diamonds, gave proof of this wealth. In the gardens there were pools filled with perfumed clear water where Princesses and their ladies in waiting could take a bath during hot days. Visitors of other realms carried the news of this extraordinary prosperity and abundance to countries all over the world and therefore the Sultan's fame was known far and wide.

Pashas bowed deep down in front of him and even Princes and Princesses, of whom there were many, would not take any decision, without consulting their father first. They respected him so much that everybody felt safe and taken care of under the absolute guidance of the Sultan.

The exception was the youngest Prince, who never seemed to be happy or satisfied. He longed to see the world, do great deeds and eventually become a great Sultan himself. The Pashas, his brothers and sisters cautioned him repeatedly, not to aggravate his father by being too rebellious. The Sultan did not allow anybody to speak or act against his will and would not hesitate to take strong measures against even his own son.

But the young Prince did not listen. He argued with the Pashas about absurd orders, continuously questioning the administrative rules and simply not following orders his father had given, if he himself did not see any good in them. As a result, there were many occasions for disagreements!

Inevitably, it happened, that one day the Sultan banished the young Prince from the castle, without any money or support whatsoever. He forced his son to live like a poor beggar, because nobody dared to give the Prince work, so he could earn at least his own daily bread.

The young fellow had no choice but to go away and leave the realm of the Sultan. Hence, one day he joined a caravan that was crossing the big dessert. And that was the last anyone had seen or heard of him.

Everybody in the castle was shocked. Not even the Princes and Princesses dared to move anymore when the Sultan was passing them in the castle. They fell on their knees, remaining motionless and only rising back up again once he had gone by. This way the Sultan continued to rule for many more years and no one spoke of the young Prince again.

That is, until one day, when the Sultan happened to fall gravely ill. A ferocious fever weakened him to such an extent that he could not give the simplest orders anymore. The Pashas waited in front of the door of his bedroom to receive answers to their questions. Answers that they needed in order to govern the regions and towns. But the Sultan's doctors shook their heads and told them to come back the following day.

The next day, however, doctors again did not allow anybody to enter the bedroom of the Sultan. There was nothing that could be done about it. The Pashas had to be patient and wait.

A queue of waiting people got longer and longer in front of the Emperor's door. Princesses and Princes, other members of the court, administrators; the whole country lined up waiting for instructions. All of them had important questions and did not dare to take a decision on their own.

With each passing day of sickness, the queue of lingering people became longer and longer. Folks waiting in anticipation, stood one behind the other, building a line along the walls of the castle, a line that circled around the market place, passed through mosques, over bridges and back, until, finally, even through the kitchen in the castle. Nobody wanted to give up their place because they were afraid of losing their position and having to start all over again at the end of the line the following day. It was a devastating sight!

The merchants at the markets were the first to close, because their customers could no longer get to the market. Even if one of them would have made it inside, it was impossible to leave again. The young boys from the bakeries, who had always carried fresh bread and buns on their heads to town, offering it to everybody along the way, could no longer wander about and sell pastry. The tea kitchens could no longer fetch water at the wells and had to stop making tea.

Eventually, it became impossible to live a normal life, because nobody could pursue his business anymore. And now, every person unable to make a living queued up for instructions from the Sultan.

Consequently, the waiting line kept growing. There was no more space in town. The queue of waiting people went out through the city gates, across the fields, over the land, getting longer and longer.

The Pashas, who were still waiting right in front of the door of the Sultan's bed room, watched the queue growing and they became very afraid. For sure, the Sultan would hold them responsible for this situation once he awoke from his fever! And then they would be in great trouble, because they had not done anything about it. But what to do? Whatever they would decide risked the wrath of the Sultan. What a terrible situation!

Day and night, they discussed among themselves what could be done to solve this difficult problem. Until, finally, one of them had the idea to bring back the young Prince.

"He has already fallen into disgrace!", the Pasha said. "He could do what he feels is right. What difference does it make to him if the Sultan gets angry with him? If it works out, it will be to our own benefit, because we have brought him back, and if not, it will be his fault!"

The Pashas liked the idea, but then wondered who of them should travel abroad to bring back the banished Prince. Not one of them was prepared to leave his precious position in the queue. Again, they argued for days, until finally they agreed on the only solution possible: all of them had to go.

When the Pashas finally stepped out of the line to pack their travel belongings, the Princes and Princesses moved up to take their places, those behind them moved up to take theirs, and those behind took a step forward as well. The whole queue began to move.

People farther down the line, who could not see what was going on in front of the line, thought that finally something was happening. And they thought that the waiting had been worthwhile, because now there was movement. Consequently, people would not give up their places for anything in the world anymore, persisting on staying put more than ever.

Meanwhile the Pashas reluctantly joined the next caravan. They followed it the way up north, the direction the youngest Prince had once taken. In every village, every little town, they asked around if anybody had seen the young Prince and what path he had taken. They followed the instructions of the people, over rivers and mountains, through distant towns, deserts and forests, foreign countries, through ice and snow, until, after a very long journey, they finally reached a foreign kingdom.

And, even though it is difficult to believe, there, in that faraway place, they actually found the young Prince!

The young lad had worked for some time in a tavern with a spring next to the house, providing exquisitely fresh water. He rented a room from the hostess and her five daughters. He had built an aqueduct from the water source right into the house, exactly, as he had known from his father's palace. That had created big excitement all over the place and people had come to ask him to build more aqueducts for their homes. Among them had been the mayor of the town. This was how the son of the mayor and the young Prince had become best of friends and the Prince no longer had wished to leave the community. The hostess and her five daughters had become his family and he loved the girls like his own sisters so far away.

One can imagine the excitement of the public when the exotic caravan with the strange looking Pashas stopped in front of the tavern. Many people came to the tavern to see what was going on, to hear what the foreign men had to say and what they wanted.

The young Prince listened attentively to the words of the Pashas. For three days and three nights he reflected upon their request. The fourth day he finally said to them:

"I have decided to go back with you to the kingdom of my father and I accept the responsibility of fixing the problem."

To his friend, the son of the mayor, he said: "Please, come with me! I would love to have you by my side. Please bring your shawm[1] along, we will need it."

The very next morning they bade farewell to their friends and families.

During the long journey back to his father's kingdom the young Prince and his friend had plenty of time to discuss the problem and how they could possibly solve it. They examined many ideas, argued about solutions, thought about the pros and cons. At night, when they were tired from the journey and debating all day, the son of the mayor played his shawm and the Prince listened to the music and told stories he came up with while listening to the melodies. Thus, they invented new stories and tunes almost every night.

The Pashas watched them with great aversion from a safe distance, smiling at them, but taking great care not to get involved in

---

[1] ancient wind instrument

these arguments. Imagine the young hothead and his friend taking care of the delicate business! Imagine they burned their fingers! They, the Pashas, would certainly stay out of it. They had done their duty!

When the caravan, after months of travelling, finally reached the kingdom of the Sultan the two friends knew exactly what they wanted to do.

The Sultan was still unconscious and the queue of the waiting was longer than ever. Nobody moved. Everything had fallen into complete immobility. Not even the birds would sing or fly anymore. They sat motionless in the trees, waiting for better times. It was a frightening scene!

But the two young lads were not to be intimidated.

"I will start at the beginning of the queue", spoke the Prince to his friend, "and you at the end. We will not stop until we have met in the middle."

And thus, they went to work.

The son of the mayor walked all the way to the end of the line and sat down. He took out his shawm and started playing the nicest tune he knew. He was careful in the beginning, but gradually he merrily played more and more.

At first, people only turned their heads, listening. It was quite an appreciated distraction during this tiring activity of total idleness.

Eventually, some of them started tapping their toes along with the rhythm, then started rocking their bodies, even whistling along.

At one point, two young girls began singing and happily clapping their hands, and two young fellows grabbed each other's shoulders and started dancing.

Seeing this reaction, the Prince's friend got encouraged even more and he started playing ever more cheerful tunes. When he ran out of melodies, he simply started playing whatever came to his mind, until everybody in the line in front of him started singing along and dancing with each other. People jumped in circles, twirled and pirouetted und turned to the music with great laughter.

And then, something incredible happened. When they were tired from dancing and singing, they decided to go home and that way, the end of the queue started dissolving. The son of the mayor continued playing his music proceeding further up the queue, until people farther up the line also started dancing and singing. That way he kept moving forward, dissolving the queue step-by-step.

Meanwhile, the Prince took his position at the beginning of the line. He sat down on a stool and began to tell a story. His first tale was about passion and love, and before long his sisters stepped out of the line to sit next to him.

The next anecdote he told was about standing up and being courageous. More people from the waiting stepped aside to listen to him. The Prince continued talking about the importance of communication, speaking and listening, about precious knowledge and all else of great value. And every time one of his stories came to an end people started asking him questions. By and by they began discussing and arguing about the messages. One interpreted it this way, his neighbor that way. And while debating, thinking and weighing the various options, some of them discovered a solution all on their own. And that, without instructions from the Sultan!

Surprised about their own capacity of coming up with solutions, they started going home to do what they had decided. The Prince took his stool and moved on to sit down again a little further down the line, where he started his story all over again.

For three days and three nights the Prince and his friend were busy playing melodies and telling stories. The fourth day, finally, they spotted each other from afar. At that point they began to combine the stories with the tunes, just like they had done during the long trip.

People loved these musical stories so much that the rest of the queue dissolved at once. The entire country started dancing, singing, clapping and discussing what they had heard. Those who did not, sat down to watch carefully and think.

Meanwhile, other musicians had joined the son of the mayor and now, they continued playing the tunes the Prince's friend had started. The brothers and sisters of the Prince were the first to repeat his tales. Gradually more and more people were discussing and reflecting on their problems. The Prince and his friend trusted they could now leave the promising development of the process to the people, knowing, that they would continue by themselves.

They went straight to the palace of the Sultan, where the Pashas were running about in great excitement.

"Handling the situation like this," they exclaimed, "we could have done it ourselves! Look at the confusion you have created! How can anybody rule this chaos? You have made everything worse than before!"

But the young Prince stood firm.

"Go back to your regions and towns and do your job!", he spoke. "You will see that people have learnt to find solutions to their problems themselves. Trust me! I will stay here and report to my father as soon as he wakes up."

For each Pasha he recruited one musician and one story teller, and asked them to support the Pashas in their duty.

The Pashas left. Some of them were happy not to be held responsible, while others thought that the musician and the story teller would keep up the spirits of the people.

The Prince and his friend, however, sat by the bed of the sick Sultan. There, they began to play soft melodies and telling wonderful stories, one after the other, even though the Sultan did not open his eyes. Day and night, they kept up this routine. When the Prince had to rest, his friend continued, and when the son of the mayor had to rest, the Prince continued.

Many days and many nights passed this way.

One morning the Sultan finally opened his eyes. As he heard the lovely music of an instrument unknown to him, he believed he had passed away. And when he saw his youngest son whom he had banished from his court years ago, he became very frightened. He believed that it was his fault that his son had died and now he was haunted by his son's spirit.

"My son!", he spoke to the Prince, "if only I could, I would give you my kingdom to make up for the wrongs I have done to you."

"Only under one condition", the young Prince laughed, because he was happy seeing his father recovered. "I will rule this kingdom together with my friend."

"Like this it shall be!", the Sultan replied, more than relieved to have overcome this evil spirit.

A couple of days later the Sultan, of course, realized that he had not passed away. But he could no longer take back his words and so he had to hand over the powers to his youngest son.

From that day on, telling stories, debating, reflecting and thinking became the most popular activity of the people in the country. Every night they met at the tea kitchens, listened to stories and discussed. And every night they returned home with new thoughts and ideas that they turned into good use the following day.

Every month the Prince and his friend sent spices, textiles, dates and salt to the kingdom far away, where their families joyfully received the goods. The camels always returned loaded with other merchandise that was produced there. Both kingdoms became wealthy and people lived happily.

And if it happened that someone came to the palace and asked for instructions, the Prince told a new story, while his friend accompanied him on his shawm.

The Magic Die

Once upon a time, in a kingdom far, far away, the king's messenger returned from a long journey to a distant land, bringing along, among other things, a mysterious object.

It was a magic die, which he had traded in for some coins from an old man at a market. But since the object would not do any tricks for him, he thought he had been cheated and gave it away as a toy to the oldest Princess and Prince, their younger siblings being too young for such a toy.

"I was told, every time you roll a six you may ask a question and you shall receive the correct answer", he laughed. "I have tried to put it to my service, but it would not work for me. Maybe you will have more luck? Have fun playing with the die!"

As soon as the messenger was out of sight, the two youngsters started rolling the die.

The Prince rolled it several times, until finally he got the desired result. He closed his eyes and asked aloud:

"What is the name of my sister?"

At that question the die opened on one side, just like a treasure box. And inside there was a small paper roll. The Prince pulled it out and read aloud to his sister:

"You have two sisters. Which sister's name are you looking for?"

"Oh! The die is very smart!", spoke the Princess. "You really have to think before asking. Now it is my turn!"

So, she rolled the die as well, until the number six turned up. She closed her eyes, thought deeply about the question and finally asked: "Which kingdom is producing the best silk?"

Again, the die opened on one side and the Princess found the answer on a tiny manuscript: "There is more than one land, far beyond the realm of the Sultan, over the mountains and beyond."

The two royal youngsters laughed with joy, grabbed each other's hands and danced around the room.

"With this die I will be the perfect Prince! Just like a true Prince is supposed to be!", he exclaimed overjoyed.

.

"And I will be the perfect Princess! Just like a true Princess is supposed to be!", added his sister.

Both of them kept their secret carefully and hid the die in a secret spot only they knew. And from that day on, every day before their daily classes they went to ask the die whatever homework they had to do. They no longer bothered to waste their time with studies or boring research on questions their teachers had given them to work on.

Soon, the teachers noticed that the Princess and the Prince had started developing great knowledge and they felt flattered, because they thought that their good teaching finally showed excellent results. Even when they started to choose more demanding tasks and more complex questions, the Princess and the Prince solved them without any difficulty.

Consequently, the teachers met to discuss among them what could be done to find new topics of interest with the most suitable questions for their eager students to work on. But as soon as they had come up with a new task for their royal students, the youngsters already came back with the result. And the answers of the Princess and the Prince were so excellent that even all the books in the royal library would have fallen silent in astonishment, if they had had the ability to speak.

It went on like this week after week, month after month and the teachers began to have serious difficulties in finding new subjects. They argued for three days and three nights about the most difficult question they could find, in order to challenge the royal children for at least a couple of days.

But what had taken the professors three days to figure out, the Princess and the Prince brilliantly answered the following day.

The scholars remained speechless.

Finally, they decided to consult the Queen and the king.

"Your highnesses", they said, "there is nothing left we can teach the Princess and the Prince anymore. They know all the answers! We can no longer teach them."

The Queen looked astonished and the King had a thoughtful expression on this face as he wondered: "Isn't that a little exaggerated?"

The Queen, however, turned to the teachers and said:

"We would like to observe for ourselves, if what you say is true. Go and find the three most difficult issues of all books. Tomorrow we will question our daughter and our son right here in the royal hall. And then we shall see!"

The scholars had quite an uneasy night fulfilling this order, but when the sun rose, they finally had found three very challenging questions. In the morning they presented the royal adolescents with a complicated mathematical task, a highly problematic philosophical issue and a historical question nobody had ever been able to answer.

But barely had the teachers left them to work out the questions, the two kids appeared in the royal hall in front of their parents with all the results. Now even the Queen and the King had to admit that the scholars had not overstated the situation.

"My dear children, I have to give you credit, indeed. You have truly improved!", the King said impressed. "Since your knowledge seems to have reached such high levels, we now have to find the best scholars in the world to teach you. Therefore, there shall be a contest and we will invite all teachers and professors from all over the kingdom. Whoever will be able to ask a question that you cannot answer, shall be your new class master."

Soon after, everybody started speaking about the extraordinarily smart Princess and Prince. Scholars, teachers and many others from countries and kingdoms far away came to court to participate in the contest. Along with them arrived many curious observers who had heard amazing stories about the famous royal youngsters and just wanted to watch the spectacle.

The castle was decorated, silverware was polished, curtains were washed and in the royal hall a little stage was put up, where the Princess and Prince should sit while answering the questions.

When the big day finally arrived, there were so many people trying to watch the two famous youngsters that the huge door had to be kept open so they could peek through it even from outside.

One scholar after the other presented the tasks and questions they had brought along.

The Princess and the Prince noted them carefully. Then they withdrew into their study right next to the royal hall to work out the solutions. But in reality, they did not waste one second and immediately rolled the magic die. Shortly after, they appeared on stage with the result they had received. Time and time again they presented perfect answers to the astonished public.

More scholars waiting in line stepped forward, presented their question and the same procedure as before repeated itself. When there was no scholar left, the royal jester jumped in front of the stage and spoke to the royal parents:

"Why don't you let me give it a try? I know of a most entertaining brain teaser, that should be great fun to all of you!"

The Queen and the King nodded in agreement, since everybody was quite fond of the jester's jokes.

So, he jumped around in circles along the line of spectators and recited:

It is a house, so small, not wide,
From six flanks you are guided inside.
Eight corners, there have always been,
one of them forever unseen.
It has been heard of in many tenses,
and is surrounded by twelve fences.
Which protect the 21 eyes,
Eternally looking outside like spies.

"Well, now?", the jester asked the Princess and Prince. He stopped right in front of them, looking at them, in anticipation of their answer, straight into their eyes.

Brother and sister glanced at each other, but none of them had a clue what the jester was talking about. They could not even withdraw to ask the magic die, because they had not understood the question in the first place. Besides, the jester would not leave them out of sight; he stood close by and moved along with them, jumping gaily around the youngsters. No matter which way they turned, he was in their face.

Everybody in the royal hall started whispering and wondering what had happened. Did the Princess and Prince not know the answer to the jester's riddle?

"We need time to think about it!", the Princess said finally.

"Fair enough!", their mother answered and rose from her throne. "So, the royal jester will be your teacher until you will know the answer."

The youngsters hurried out of the royal hall, but the jester followed them right behind. They tried to get rid of the annoying fellow by hurrying along the castle's hallways, quickly turning right, then suddenly left and right again. They opened and closed doors, hurried up and down stairs, rushed around corners, but the jester followed them as if he had been glued to their feet.

Finally, the Prince stopped and turned around to speak to him: "If you do not mind, we would like to withdraw to think and discuss your riddle!"

But the jester simply jumped around them, happily clapping his hands and singing:

Discussing the riddle, there is no need!
The answer is found in a truly funny deed!

Thus, the jester stayed proximate to them until they had to close their bedroom doors to go to sleep. But already early in the morning he waited outside the door. The royal youngsters had no opportunity at all to ask the die.

By then, everybody in the kingdom had heard about the riddle that the brilliant royal children should solve. Some even thought to have found the answer themselves and people started arguing about it in the town's tavern or at the market. They bet their money on the answer they believed to be the right one and therefore waited anxiously for the final result from the Princess and the Prince. Surely, they could be trusted to give the correct answer, since until that day they had known all the answers.

Meanwhile the Princess and the Prince had become quite desperate. They had tried in vain to sneak away in an unobserved moment. But the jester never failed to pay full attention to them.

They had even tried unsuccessfully to solve the riddle themselves, but since they were so out of practice, no good idea would come to their minds.

Three days and three nights had already gone by and still they had no clue. How embarrassing would it be if the whole world learned about their failure. The perfect royal children would no longer be perfect, burdened with shame and disdain, rejected by the entire world. How could they rule a kingdom one day, if everybody thought poorly of them? The more they thought about it, the more distressed they became.

"Only you can help us out of this miserable situation!", they finally said to the jester at the end of the fourth day. "Please tell us the answer to the riddle! We do not know it."

"Very well", he jubilated, jumping around the two youngsters.

"You may listen to my answer, no concern,
But tell me, what is there to get in return?"

The Princess and the Prince thought about it. Finally, the Princess offered him her precious ring, made of pure gold. And the Prince took off his belt with shining silver adornments.

But the jester shook his head.

"Want no silver and no gold,
Wit and laughter should be told!"

The youngsters looked at each other in despair.

"We have a magic die! You shall have it, if you help us out of this awful situation. It has caused us only trouble," the Princess said at least.

"A magic die?!", exclaimed the jester in joy clapping his hands. "That sounds like fun!"

And he agreed to help them.

The royal youngsters lead him to the hidden place.

"Let us roll the die one last time!", begged the Prince. "Then it shall be yours forever."

The Princess rolled the number six on her first attempt. She closed her eyes and recited:

"It is a house, so small, not wide,

From six flanks you are guided inside.

Eight corners, there have always been,

one of them forever unseen.

It has been heard of in many tenses,

and is surrounded by twelve fences.

Which protect the 21 eyes,

Eternally looking outside like spies.

She took out the little paper role and read:

"That is me!"

As soon as she said these words, the die began to dance wildly around the room. The Princess tried to catch it with her hands. The Prince jumped up and threw himself on the floor in order to get a hold of it. Even the jester chased it in vain and ended up on the floor together with the royal youngsters, the die still dancing around them like it was teasing them.

The die continued to bounce and twirl and finally landed on the tip of the jester's nose, spinning like a twister. He burst out in laughter and could not get a hold of it, because the die tickled him fiercely.

Seeing the jester in that situation, the Princess began to giggle, because it was too funny to watch. Soon also her brother was holding his tummy, shaking with laughter. Finally, all three of them were rolling on the floor with tears of laughter.

Everybody in the castle suddenly stopped with whatever they were doing: The Queen and King stopped signing documents and giving orders, the cook stood motionless without stirring the soup and the blacksmith held his hammer high, not letting it beat the hot iron. The more they giggled, the more people became curious in the entire castle.

At that point the die opened up, just like it wanted to produce an answer. But this time it simply poured out black pepper right onto the noses of the three.

Now the jester and the two youngsters started sneezing and they ended up sneezing and laughing and giggling and sneezing again and again they could not stop however much they tried.

Meanwhile the Queen and the King, followed by the entire court, rushed to the hidden room in the tower to find out the reason for this unusual disturbance.

When they opened the door, they were puzzled by a very peculiar scene. The noses of the Princess and Prince and even the jester's were totally black and their cheeks were wet with tears, while all three of them were rolling around on the floor, chased by a die swirling around them, as if they were in the centre of a cyclone.

The Prince was the first to find his speech again.

"The answer to the riddle is that the die is perfect, because it teaches us that fear and tear and laughter are one and the same. It rescued us from the slavery of perfection."

And his sister added: "The jester was an excellent teacher. We have learnt an important lesson! But now we wish to go back to the classes with our tutors."

Nobody understood the answer of the Prince, which was even more enigmatic than the original riddle.

But the jester nodded in agreement:

"Being perfect in magic forever,
will hide the truth, you'll find it never!"

From that day on people in the castle, in the town's tavern and at the market kept on guessing what the puzzling words of the three could mean. Nobody won a bet and for years people kept trying to interpret the meaning over and over again.

Even today, it still happens that someone brings up the riddle once more and everybody starts guessing all over again.

The Blue Key

Once upon a time, the royal messenger arrived galloping at the town's tavern. Her message was so urgent that she did not even get off her horse to inform the inn keepers of the planned arrival of some very important persons. A Princess with her entire entourage from a foreign kingdom was expected and consequently, there was not enough room in the castle. So, three persons had to be placed in the very best rooms of the tavern.

However, the innkeeper, a widow with her five daughters, was away to purchase new supplies and had left the house to the girls, who were all old enough to run the business on their own.

The lady messenger was hardly out of sight, when the five daughters grabbed each other's hands, dancing joyfully in circles.

"What great honour for our house!", they exclaimed and, "Our mother will be so proud of us, when she returns and discovers how well we have managed a challenging situation with such honourable guests!"

Immediately each one of them rushed off in a different direction, in order to start preparations. The oldest took out the special silverware to polish it. The second searched the storage room for excellent ingredients for cooking. The third took down the dusty curtains to get washed. The fourth started scrubbing the tables, the floor and the stairs and the youngest hurried to the wine cellar to get out the finest bottles for the special guests.

But the young girl found the heavy wooden door locked. She searched for the key behind the stone, where their mother usually kept it, but it was not there. She looked more closely around her, but could not find it. She hurried back into the house and checked all the drawers, cupboards, shelves, looked even in dishes and behind plates. But the key was not to be found anywhere.

At that point she called her four sisters to the door, from which four steps were leading down to the wine cellar.

"Look! The door is locked, we cannot get out the good wine!", she informed them.

The oldest sister stood at the top of the four stairs and answered: "Certainly our mother has taken the key along with her on her trip. She will have good reason to do so. Now, why should we worry? Our mother knows what she is doing."

The second sister stood on the second step and said: "Not to worry, little sister! It's not worth it! We will serve the cheap wine in fine silver cups and nobody will notice."

The third sister, who had stopped on the third step, shrugged her shoulders and crossed her arms in front of her chest saying: "I understand very well why you are troubled, but there is nothing we can do about it. We do not have the key and without the key we cannot open the door."

The youngest girl finally turned to the fourth sister, who stood on the last step, closest to her. But she also shook her head, whining: "What can I do about it!? Our three older sisters do not have any advice and you expect me to know what to do?!"

"Leave it!", the oldest daughter interrupted putting an end to the discussion. "Let's get back to work. That is more important!"

But the youngest did not follow her sisters back into the house. She remained in front of the closed door, gazing intently at the lock and considering her options to solve this problem.

Finally, she decided to ask her friend's father, the blacksmith, to make a second key. He listened to her suggestion but shook his head.

"I can only copy a key if I have the mold of the original", he said. "But I know who might be able to help you."

"Who is it? Tell me!", the young girl demanded, as he hesitated to speak his mind.

"Well", he reluctantly continued, "I do not know from my own experience, I can only tell what I have heard from others."

"Whatever it is, I will try it!", the youngest daughter exclaimed.

"Among us blacksmiths there is this tale about a sorceress, who lives up in the mountains, at the old iron mine", he told. "The story goes, that she has great powers. But it is also said that she loves solitude and gets angry when disturbed."

"I will try anyway!", the girl repeated firmly.

"But it is very far. You will have to walk for one day and one night!"

"We better take our donkey, father!", said the girl's friend, who had been standing by listening in astonishment, to what his father had said. "I will come along to help her."

So, the youngest daughter and the blacksmith's son set out on the donkey the same day. There was no time to be wasted, because the guests were expected soon.

They were riding for many hours and rested only briefly to let the donkey drink fresh water at a clear mountain creek. They climbed a narrow, winding path. At each turn, each junction, each change of direction they hoped to finally see the old mine. But at every turn they were disappointed and had to hike even further, until after countless turns they finally reached the cold zone above the tree line where snow covers the ground year-round. But at last they arrived in front of the old mine, just like the blacksmith had said.

They tied the donkey to a bush in a protected area, so it could rest while they were looking for the sorceress.

"Where might this magician lady live? Up here it's cold and icy! No one can seriously live up here?!", the young girl wondered.

But hardly had she spoken these words, her friend pointed to an entrance of a cave a little uphill from the spot where they were standing.

They climbed up and entered a tunnel, that seemed to be leading straight inside the ice. There was shining blue and glittering silver and shimmering green everywhere around them. It was the most beautiful sight they had ever seen.

Carefully they went on until they reached a hall with walls made of snow. At the ceiling were windows of clear ice, allowing golden sun beams to brighten the entire place. In the middle of the room stood a table made of dazzling white snow. Bluish ice and silver flowers decorated the walls around them. At the ceiling there were thousands of ice crystals, touching lightly as if there were a breeze –

which wasn't the case - and thus creating a mysterious sound.

The two young people stood in astonishment with open mouths, looking at this marvel and for a moment forgetting all about the reason why they had come.

"It's been a while since I had guests", a voice suddenly spoke behind their backs.

Fearfully they turned around and found the sorceress standing right in front of them. She wore a long, blue dress and a dark blue cloak. On her head she balanced a pointed blue, green and silver hat, sparkling just like the ice around them.

"We do not want to disturb", the young girl answered anxiously.

"I would appreciate it if more guests visited", the sorceress replied and offered them a seat at the table. "Only few take the trouble to come up here. They rather make up wild stories about me, that create fear of me, so they have a good reason not to climb the mountain. Most people are indeed rather cowardly. So, why have you come up here to see me?"

Quickly the girl told her about her predicament with the key.

The ice woman nodded with pointed lips, saying a lot of "hm's" while listening and wandering up and down in front of the table. The girl and her friend followed her movements closely with their eyes.

Then the ice woman stopped abruptly and spoke: "I will make this key for you. But I will need five long hairs of young girls. A white one and a black one, one brown, one golden, and also a red hair. But these hairs need to be fresh, so you will have to bring the girls up here. Otherwise the magic will not work."

As fate had it, all five sisters had long, beautiful strong hair of exactly the required colors. The hair of the eldest daughter was so light, it almost seemed white. The second daughter had shiny dark hair, almost as black as coal. The third had brown hair like hazelnuts and the fourth hair of gold, just like the sun. The youngest herself, had curls so red it almost seemed unreal.

Immediately the two friends made their way back down the mountain.

As the young girl entered the tavern, she found her sisters occupied with their various chores.

The eldest stood behind the counter, looking motionless at some silver cups she had lined up in front of her. With an absent smile she moved one after the other into the light to check the reflection of the material.

The second sister sat at the table, sorting green peas from chick peas. There was a huge pile in front of her. She counted aloud as she busily pushed the green peas to one side and the chick peas to the other.

Meanwhile her third sister was beating her fourth sister with a towel and yelled: "Leave the broom! We need to wash the curtains! That is much more important."

And the poor sister, punished for no apparent reason, only answered "Very well, very well! We'll do it!" and tried to escape, running around the furious sister.

"My dear sisters! Listen to me", the youngest said and told them about the sorceress on the mountain, who would make another key to the wine cellar for them, on condition that they brought her the requested hairs.

She went to her oldest sister, grabbed both of her hands, saying: "Our dear mother could not have foreseen that we would have such high-born guests. Surely, she would not have taken the key along with her, if she had anticipated that!"

These words made the eldest think.

And to the second sister she spoke: "What good is the purest food, if the wine served is of poor quality?"

At this, the second daughter, too paused, looking pensively.

As for the third sister, she took away the towel from her and spoke: "Stop beating our sister! Such aggression has never produced any good! Rather comb her hair, so they will be clean and shiny when we get there."

The third sister put her fists on her hips, pondering and grunting, but she stopped hitting her sister.

Finally, the youngest handed the towel to the fourth sister and demanded: "Stop whining! Whining has never got anybody anywhere. Go and get two donkeys from our neighbors so all of us can ride up the mountain!"

"You must be kidding?!", replied the eldest daughter and the three other sisters nodded heavily in agreement. "And who will take care of all the work here, while we are away?"

"Who else has such wonderfully white hair as you, such hazelnut brown hair as you, such golden hair like you or such black hair as you?", the youngest replied, pointing from one sister to the other.

The girls had to admit that this was indeed an exceptional occurrence and they did not know of anybody else who could fulfill the requested requirements so perfectly. So, they gave in and agreed to make their way up the mountain.

They followed the same winding path, turn after turn, uphill to the snow fields and the pointed rocks. The girls looked in amazement with open mouths as their youngest sister led them into the ice hall. Once inside she tore one long hair off each sister's head and lay them out on the table. A white one, a black, another brown, one golden and at last one of her own red hair.

As soon as the last hair was put on the table, the ice woman appeared.

She swirled her magic stick over the girl's hairs. Miraculously the ice crystals over their heads started singing a magical sound.

The five hairs started twisting around each other in circles and began to form the shape of a key. Pure fine snow started coming down from the ceiling and laid softly on the fragile new key, until it was all covered by white snowflakes.

The sorceress examined her work and found it to her satisfaction. Then she sprinkled some ice water over the key, until it was perfectly covered by a solid transparent coat. At last she placed the delicate item on a little ice tray before finally handing the brilliant object over to the girls.

"This key will open the door", she spoke. "But you have to get home before sunrise, otherwise the key will melt!"

The five sisters thanked the magician.

Quickly they wrapped the cold key into a cloth and collected snow to create a big snow ball around it to keep it cool. The snowball then was put into a large blanket, tied to a long stick, that had been useful on the way up, and packed it on the backs of the two donkeys. Thus, the two animals transported the valuable item between them down the path towards the valley.

But time was precious, and the girls hurried the poor beasts to move faster and faster, until, all of a sudden, the snowball slipped out of the blanket and rolled down the side of the hill.

In great shock the five sisters stared at this accident and held their cheeks in fearful tremor. On and on the snow ball went downhill and became bigger and bigger and would not stop. It rolled on until it disappeared in the darkness.

"Now everything is ruined! I knew it, we should have stayed at home! Now, what have we got?!", the eldest complained.

„Well, easy come, easy go", the second only said and shrug her shoulders. "Let's go home!"

„You should not have spurred the donkeys that much! These animals are simply too stupid!", the third sister exclaimed and angrily she started beating the poor animals again, so they bolted in an attempt to flee. Eventually they managed to free themselves and ran away.

"Oh my! Oh my!", the fourth sister whined: "Now we are totally lost in this cold, icy wilderness!"

And she sat down in the snow and hid her face in her arms.

But at this very moment a thundering voice came down to them from above, where the entrance to the ice hall was: "You ungrateful creatures! That is how you treat my gift to you!? You do not deserve my support!"

And with these words the sorceress appeared out of nowhere right in front of their noses. Angrily she swayed her magic stick in the direction of the eldest daughter.

Before any of them realized what was happening, the ice woman turned the girl into a rabbit as white as her hair. Then she pointed the stick towards the second sister and turned her as well into a black rabbit. And equally she proceeded with the third and the fourth sister.

The youngest, however, had not watched these terrible actions passively, but had grabbed the ice tray the key had been presented on.

"Follow me, my sisters!", she yelled and before the magician could turn around to point her magic stick at her, she swung herself onto the tray and rode it down the hill like she was sitting on a sleigh, going in the same direction the snow ball had taken earlier.

Quickly she was out of sight of the ice woman.

The four rabbits hopped after her.

It was a very wild sleigh ride through deep snow and dark trees, but the youngest daughter steered the unusual device precisely along the path the big snow ball had created.

The ball had finally come to a stop in a green meadow, where only a little snow remained, and the air was warmer. But due to the wild ride the youngest daughter did not see it right away in the darkness of the night and thus, crashed full speed right into it. The tray sailed through the air and she herself ended up stuck head over heels buried deeply in the snow ball.

But she immediately crawled out and wiped the snow off her clothes.

"We have to get the key out of this big pile of snow!", she said to herself, but it was too big for her to dig it out with her bare hands.

"Come here, my rabbits! Here I am!", she called her sisters. After a while the four rabbits finally came hopping out of the darkness and stopped in front of her feet.

"You need to dig a tunnel with your paws!", the youngest said to the bunnies. "A tunnel big enough, so I can put my arm in and grab the key!"

Straightaway the animals started digging and shoveling snow with such power and speed that it seemed to snow in the meadow. Working together, it did not take very long before they found the ice key.

Again the girl wrapped the key in a cloth and covered it with snow. But this time she carried it downhill with her own hands, very carefully, followed by the four rabbits.

The little procession reached the town right in time for the breaking dawn. The snow in the cloth had already started melting and water was dripping along the way as they hurried towards their house.

Even more water was dripping down onto the four stairs to the wine cellar door. In amazement the girl watched the water miraculously washing the steps as clean as the ice castle's stairway.

Stepping down these shiny steps, the youngest cautiously took out the key and inserted it with much care into the lock. It fitted perfectly, better than the original iron key that always got stuck. Carefully she turned it three times towards the left.

The door creaked open.

As the girl stepped inside the wine cellar, followed by the four bunnies, each one of her sisters miraculously turned back into their human shape. Happily, the girls grabbed their hands and laughed in relieved joy.

Then they picked the best wine they could find in the cellar. Meanwhile the key in the lock had melted in the warm sun and as soon as they stepped outside, the door closed with a great bang behind them.

They went back to finish all other errands that had to be done before the guests would arrive. The following day when the guests showed up as expected, everything was prepared to their best abilities. Nothing was missing; it was perfect.

After a couple of days, when their mother returned, they proudly reported to her how well all five of them had taken care of these royal guests. Their mother wanted to hear all the details of this adventure and together the six women talked until late into the night.

After this adventure, life returned to normal, as if nothing out of the ordinary had ever happened, except for a new bubbling spring of the clearest water that had formed right next to the four steps. The water was of such excellent quality not to be found anywhere else.

Eventually people from all over the country came to visit the tavern with the fresh water source. The girls named the tavern "The Bubbling Spring" and it became a famous place for pilgrims from all over the world.

Even today, with luck, this tavern may still be found. Although nobody knows exactly where it is, it still happens that a wanderer unexpectedly stumbles on the source of the bubbling spring.

The Enchanting Water Fairy

Once upon a time there was a wealthy farmer who owned a big farming estate. He had two children: a daughter with long black hair that reflected the sun like the finest silk, and a son who had equally beautiful dark hair. Both children had almond-shaped eyes, inherited from their mother. Because of this, people always recognized them immediately as brother and sister, for in this kingdom almond-shaped eyes were not common.

The estate gave work to many people and there were numerous servants. Nevertheless, as soon as the children were old enough, the farmer had made them work on the farm. At an early age, he instructed his son to act as the leader of the servants and field workers, ordering them what to do and controlling the finances. The young man loved to count the daily produce and to note everything efficiently in his books. Whenever he had some spare time he would stroll through the barns and cellars and look with the utmost satisfaction at the abundant assets.

His sister, on the other hand, had been instructed to work just like the maids, keeping the house clean, washing vegetables, cooking meals for everybody, and at night repairing torn clothes. She did not appreciate her duties too much, but still carried them out thoroughly anyway. She loved working in the garden, taking excellent care of the fruit trees. Whenever she had some spare time she would go there and look happily at the healthy trees laden with fruits.

The farmer's wife had passed away at a young age, and the farmer had never re-married. And much too soon, he died as well. He left the thriving farming estate to both his children, who by then had become young adults. The daughter received as her part of the heritage the garden with the fruit trees. The son inherited the farmhouse and all the estate's buildings, with the land and the fields, as well as the livestock. All the workers and maids had to work exclusively for him from that day on.

After the funeral ceremony the young man said to his sister: "Now you cannot live here anymore. It is no longer your home. Your property is the garden. Be sure to build yourself a home there and make your own living! The farming estate is my property now."

The girl sadly went into the garden and built herself a bed of leaves underneath the biggest tree. Before she went to sleep, she strolled to the little pond at the edge of the garden, looked at the calm water and sighed:

"What shall become of me now?"

Then she turned around and went to lie down on her bed of leaves.

For seven nights it went on like this and it almost started becoming a habit to her. But the last night, looking over the water, she discovered an unbelievable creature, spinning over the surface of the water as if it was a dance floor. It was a young woman entirely made of water drops, dancing with great joy over the surface of the little pond.

The farmer's daughter believed to be dreaming. So, she pinched herself, but the beautiful being was still there.

„Do not distrust what you see", the young water woman spoke to her. "I am real."

„You are the most beautiful individual I have ever seen!", the girl said in admiration of the exceptional beauty of her figure, her delicate face and her fine gestures, now that she could observe her more closely.

"That is nothing out of the ordinary for fairies", the creature laughed. "You know, I am a water fairy. But thank you anyway for your kind words. We do not hear that too often, because people think it's not necessary to tell us."

"If you really are a fairy, may I spend some time with you?", the farmer's daughter asked. "I am all alone and longing for company."

„I would be very happy if you stayed with me for a while", the fairy replied and danced in a large circle over the water. "The only thing is, I cannot leave the pond. You need to come here onto the water with me, if you wish to have my to be with me."

Hesitating, the girl looked at the water.

"I wish I could dance like you", she said.

"But nothing easier than that!", the fairy answered. "Come back tomorrow at the same time. Now it is too late, as I soon will have to return to the bottom of the lake."

That night the farmer's daughter slept well.

The next day she picked many baskets of fruit and sold them at the market. At dusk she went to the pond. Right on time, because, just as the sun went down behind the horizon and the sky turned the color of the water red, the fairy appeared.

She reached out her hand to the farmer's daughter and led her onto the surface of the water. With the utmost surprise the young girl gazed at her feet as they were walking over the water without sinking in. She dared her first steps and then followed the fairy in her moves. Thus, the fairy and the girl danced until it became dark and the fairy had to go again. The following night they repeated the process and so it went many times. During daytime the farmer's daughter picked fruits, sold them at the market and at dusk she fervently learnt how to dance, taught by the water fairy. Her days and evenings were so filled with passionate things to do that she forgot all about her distress.

One night the fairy finally spoke to her: "You have learnt very well. You dance just as fine as I do. As a gift for your open-mindedness I will give you this dress. Look after it well, because it will allow you to dance in your world just as fine as here on the water with my support."

She handed the farmer's daughter a silver dress made of shiny water drops, elegantly embroidered with river pearls.

"I thank you with all my heart!", the young girl exclaimed and put on the garment immediately. She turned around, dancing in circles, gazing at the marvelous way the dress swirled around her body, and so overfilled with joy over the amazing gift, that she did not notice that she was dancing all by herself. After a while she paused, taking a breath and looking out for the water fairy. But the fairy was no longer there, even though it was not yet dark.

So, the farmer's daughter took off the valuable dress, folding it carefully into a blanket, so it would not dry in the sun and kept it safe underneath the big cherry tree.

She continued to go to the pond night after night. But the water fairy would not return anymore. After three nights of waiting she finally decided to put on the dress and dance alone.

"The fairy has taught me to dance", she assured herself. "I have learnt well! And I will continue to do it by myself and be happy about it."

From that day on she went every evening to the pond and danced in her beautiful dress, all alone.

One night a young farmer's son, who was known in the entire kingdom for the delicious golden honey he sold, happened to pass by. He was looking for a new place to put up more of his bee hives. Immediately enchanted by the sight of this beautiful girl, dancing in a dress more exquisite and dazzling than that of a Princess, he stopped.

"How breathtaking you look in this gown!", he said frankly.

The farmer's daughter paused her movements to see who had come at this late hour of the day, uttering these unexpected words.

Like everybody else in the kingdom, she recognized the young lad, because at the farming estate they had always bought honey from him.

"Thank you", she replied. "Yes, the dress is quite exceptional. I love it very much!"

The young men asked her, if he could place a few of his bee hives in her fruit garden, and willingly, she showed him the way.

The following evening, she heard the same voice again: "You really dance beautifully!"

Again, she interrupted her dancing and looked at the young man.

"Thank you", she replied like the first time. "Yes, I have practiced a lot and I try to keep up with what I have learnt."

This time the young lad asked if he could have a look at his bee hives and see if the population was happy with the place. And again, she willingly showed him the way into her garden.

But when she heard his voice again the third night, proclaiming "you dance beautifully in this stunning outfit!", she turned to the young man and answered:

"I appreciate your kind words. But I would like to know why you keep coming here; is it because you like to keep me company?"

The young fellow was a little embarrassed and nodded timidly.

"Certainly, I would very much like to keep you company. If I may?"

She smiled at him and so, every evening from then on, he visited her in her garden and brought her some honey. The cherry crop ended, followed by the apples, and later on the plums. Together they made sweet juice out of honey and fallen fruits that could not be sold at the market anymore. Everybody who bought their honey or fruits, tasted the sweet temptation and soon there was great demand and they had to produce more of it. Within a short period of time they became dear friends and when winter came over the land, they celebrated their wedding.

The following spring, they built a new farmhouse at the edge of the pond, almost the size of the old farmhouse, now belonging to her brother. When the construction was finished, they invited everybody to a great feast.

Her brother came with his bride, who now lived with him at the old estate. There was much food and dancing and laughter. In the evening, the farmer's daughter put on her precious dress and everybody admired how gracefully she danced to the music. When her brother noticed his sister's superb garment and how she let the fabric shine in her dance, he demanded to know where she had found such fabulous vestment. So, she reported to him exactly how it had happened.

The brother listened carefully. He found it unacceptable that his own bride would not have an equally valuable dress, if not better. He decided to go to the pond as well and get an even prettier gown for his bride.

Seven evenings in a row he stood there and sighed: "What shall become of me?"

And, sure enough, the last time he spoke these words the water fairy appeared. Just as his sister had told him, she moved gracefully over the water; in his mind she was the most beautiful creature he had ever seen. But thinking that everybody knew that fairies had to be pretty, he thought it was not worth mentioning.

"There you are!", he exclaimed instead. "I have been waiting for you! You are the water fairy, correct?"

The water lady paused her dance right in front of him and nodded friendly. "Yes, that's me. Do you need company, because you are alone?"

The young man crossed his arms over his chest.

"Alone? No! I am used to doing everything all by myself! I do not need company!", he replied and then asked straight away what he had come for: "But you can teach me how to dance!" With this he hoped to get the desired garment for his bride.

"Very well", the fairy answered. "Do come back tomorrow, at the same time. Now it is too late, and I have to go back onto the bottom of the pond."

The next day he was quite moody and fretful and querulously yelled at the servants. Finally, when evening came, he hurried impatiently to the pond.

Right on time, when the sun set over the horizon, turning the color of the water to red, the water fairy appeared. She stretched her hand out to him and guided him onto the surface of the water. The young man, who only knew about counting and controlling numbers, had a very hard time setting one foot over the other and soon lost true interest in learning. He started faking and simply copied the moves of the fairy in order to please her. He thought, this way he would get the desired gown faster. Who needed to learn such a useless thing as dancing! He already knew everything that was important to know in life.

The fairy spent a lot of time with him and only when the night came, she told him: "You have done great for the first day!"

But again, the young man crossed his arms over his chest and shrugged his shoulders: "That's nothing! It is not worth mentioning!

You should not stop before I know how to dance better than the Prince himself!"

The following evenings he came back to look for the fairy, faking interest in wanting to learn how to dance, but deep down inside he only had the precious gown in mind. Every time, when the fairy had to go, she gave him credit for his efforts and every time he would cross his arms over his chest, shrug his shoulders and reply: "That's nothing! Don't even mention it! You should not stop before I know how to dance better than the Prince himself!"

The seventh night the fairy did not show up. And also, the night after he waited in vain. That made the young man very angry, because he had not yet received the dress as a gift for his endeavors. Furiously he stomped up and down along the shore of the little lake and called for the water fairy.

"That was not the deal!", he yelled and paced in anger back and forth. "Look here, you water witch! I cannot dance like a true Prince yet! You have failed! Look, how clumsy I am!"

At this, the water fairy actually appeared. But this time she was not dancing and laughing but looked at him with sad eyes.

"You need to teach me how to dance perfectly and then give me my gift for my accomplishments! That's how it goes!", the young farmer demanded. "That is the way is has to be! You teach me and then you give me the most precious garment ever, made of silver and pearls. You cannot leave before you have fulfilled your promise! That is the deal!"

But the fairy still only looked at him in silence.

Then she spoke: "The gown does not yet suit you."

"What?!", the young man yelled and grabbed the skirt of the water fairy. "If you do not want to give it to me, I will simply take it!"

And with this he pulled at the water fairy's dress.

But when he touched it, it dissolved into a million of water drops and he fell head over heels into the pond. When he resurfaced out of the water, gasping for air, he was covered all over with pond weeds and mud. He crawled out, on to the shore and walked back to his house, grumbling and brooding, all dirty and covered in dark mud.

When the servants and his bride saw a scary looking creature coming up towards the house, they did not recognize him and ran away screaming, because they thought he was a ghost. When he finally reached his home, nobody was there anymore to serve on him. And since he never had learnt to do things for himself, he did not even know how to start a fire or do the simplest errands. Angrily he waited for the servants and his bride to return, thinking of ways to punish and teach them a lesson, so that they wouldn't dare to run away ever again.

Many days passed, many weeks, even months, and the farmer's son still waited angrily for the laborers to return so he could tell them that they had failed him miserably. The farming estate fell into disrepair, the fields grew weeds, and thorn bushes eventually grew over the walls and the buildings. The more the estate became neglected, the less the farmer's son was seen around. In the end people started telling that it was a haunted place and one better kept at a distance. At that point nobody even came close to the farming estate anymore. Everybody tried to avoid the place, and nobody could actually say what had become of the once wealthy farmer's son.

The new farming estate on the other side of the little pond, however, developed nicely. Soon after the big wedding feast a child was born and over the years there was much laughter of many children around the place. At night, when these kids went to bed, their mother told them the story of the water fairy. And for very special occasions she even took out the precious dress to dance by the pond. And if one listened very carefully, one could hear a silver laughter from afar and, a dark grumbling coming from the old farm house.

Courage Challenged

Once upon a time there lived a wealthy miller, who was called the Miller of the South, because he owned a big mill in the south of the kingdom. He had only one son, whom he loved dearly. His wife had passed away giving birth to this only child, and therefore ever since, he had had to manage all the work in the house and the mill alone, and so had little time for his son. For that reason, he had always fulfilled all the child's wishes that money could buy.

When his son had become a young man, the miller bought him a splendid horse, as fine as the horses of the royal Prince and Princess. Many girls in the kingdom spoke with great admiration of the miller's son, whenever he passed them on horseback, proud like a peacock, and not even casting a glance in their direction. But secretly he absorbed the attention he got with a never fulfilled greed.

One fine day the miller's son gathered his friends around him.

There was the son of the chocolate bakers, who had been his oldest friend since school. His skin was as dark as the chocolate his parents produced and he was the only one speaking two languages. Then, there were the two sons of the town's administrator, who were his friends, because they, too, had horses. And there was the daughter of the seamstress. She was his favorite friend. Her parents had come from a land far away and had built a fine business in town. Her skin was not as dark as that of the chocolate bakers' family, but not as light as his own and he thought that she was the most beautiful girl around and that she would make a fine match for him. Finally, there was the blacksmith's son, who had been his most faithful friend and who had always regarded him highly for his horse and the admiration he got from the girls.

"It's such a beautiful day, today!" he said to his friends. "I would love to go horseback riding with you. What do you say? We have three horses and are six. Each horse can carry two of us."

The young people liked the idea very much. They had never done anything like this before and it sounded wonderful.

So, each one of them prepared a bag with a few snacks to munch on, saddled the horses and set out into the fields. The daughter of the seamstress sat in front of the miller's son on his horse. He was very proud to hold and protect her from falling off. And she let him do it, even though she was experienced enough to sit on a horse by herself.

Feeling as happy as could be they rode off across the fields, laughing and singing, and enjoying the wonderful day. When they approached the woods, the miller's son suddenly stopped his horse.

"Who dares to ride into the forest with me?", he asked, challenging his friends playfully.

Everybody knew that this forest was the home of an evil dragon. Nobody ever went there if it could be avoided.

The group of friends hesitated.

"Now we will see who has the courage to follow me!", exclaimed the miller's son with his head held high, giving his horse the spurs.

At this point the eldest of the brothers remembered a task he had promised his father to take care of this morning. That was why he was the first to speak.

"Unfortunately, I cannot go any farther with you. You go on and have fun! I leave my horse with you. I have to go back to town and do what my father has asked me, otherwise I will get into trouble tonight."

The miller's son made a grim face.

"There we go!", he said dryly. "Now we know who the biggest coward is!"

And when the young man shrugged his shoulders, turned around and started walking back the way they had come, he yelled after him: "One like you shall no longer be my friend!"

Then he turned to the rest of the little group and asked: "Well? Who of you has the guts to accept this challenge of courage?"

All of them decided to take the path into the dark forest together.

After only a few steps the leaves of the trees became so dense that they did not allow the sun to come through anymore. They pulled their jackets tighter around their bodies, because it was cool there.

Silently they moved on, listening to the cracking sound the horses made passing through the trees and bushes, once passing a trunk on the left, then on the right.

After a while the son of the chocolate bakers started feeling very guilty, because he had promised his parents to never ever enter this woodland. And now, this was exactly what he was doing! He felt increasingly bad about it. So, finally he said:

"You folks continue. I have given my word of honour to my mother not to go into this forest. I should not disobey her! I am very sorry, but it is better to keep my promise. I will go back."

Again, the miller's son grimaced:

"There you have it!", he said with biting sarcasm. "Another coward! Go whining to your mommy! One like you shall no longer be my friend!"

While the son of the chocolate bakers made his way back out of the woods, the others continued in the opposite direction. They rode in even greater silence than before and listened to every sound that came out of the dark. There was tension, because all of them were a little afraid of the dragon.

At a creek they stopped for a short rest.

"Hold on tightly to the reins!", the miller's son said to his most faithful friend, the son of the blacksmith. "Horses have excellent hearing. They can catch the slightest noise of the dragon and may bolt, even though he might be far away."

Then they sat down on the green moss and ate their bread and fruits.

After a good rest the younger son of the town administrator suggested: "Now let's go back. It has been a nice adventure. We should not overdo it."

But the miller's son would not hear about it: "Why, no! The fun has only just started! We still have plenty of time before the sun will go down! Let's go on a little further!"

But when they came back to the spot where they had left the horses, only one horse was still waiting there. The horse of the miller's son and that of the eldest brother were gone. It upset the miller's son very much and he called his faithful friend a great fool.

"You have not fastened the reins as tightly, as I had told you! Now see, what you have done! You are not good for anything! You had better go back home, you are only a burden to us in this adventure!"

His cautious friend sadly threw his bag over his shoulder without saying a word and went off, his head down low. But the tailor's daughter would not stand by passively this time. She raised her voice.

„It is not right to speak in this way!", she said calmly. "If you send him away, I will go as well!"

Since he had wanted to impress her especially, he now felt offended by the girl and treated in an ungrateful way.

"Only a female can say such simple-minded things!", he replied. "So what, if you chose not to be my friend anymore! Watch me, how little I care!"

This is how it happened that only the youngest of the two brothers remained with him.

„All the better!", the miller's son proclaimed. "We only have one horse left and this way the two of us may share the saddle comfortably."

But now, his only friend left started worrying about his horse. He tried to reason with the miller's son.

"I do not want to risk my horse as well. We have already lost two. Let's take back my stallion and then we can come back and continue on foot. The forest is becoming too dense to make any progress with animals anyway."

But this made the miller's son even madder.

"That is only an excuse and a bad one at that!", he screamed. "I will no longer wait! A liar like you shall no longer be my friend!"

He grabbed his bag and stomped off into the forest, leaving his last friend behind. Furiously he went on, filled with pride, mumbling angrily, with his head full of annoying thoughts.

After a while he noticed that there was complete silence around him. Not even the birds were singing anymore. It was so dark that it felt almost like deep at night. Only then he realized that he had been walking without paying any attention to where he was going nor what time it was, and that he surely must have ended up close to the dragon.

At that thought he stopped, looking around carefully, not daring to breathe. It was so dark, surely, night must have fallen already. But now it was too late to turn around. He had to find a place to sleep, but his blanket and his food had been lost together with his horse.

He was cold.

And he was hungry, too.

He had nothing left, only the clothes he was wearing. Not even one friend left that could have kept him company or with whom he could have kept warm. If the dragon found him now, defenseless as he was, it would surely be his end!

He started shaking all over his body.

He sank down on his knees and started crying. He had not wanted a situation like that! First, he cried silently into his arms, then his sobs became louder and louder.

"Who goes chasing a dragon should be prepared to meet one!", a thundering voice said way above him.

"What? Who's there?"

The young lad jumped to his feet and wiped away his tears. But he could not see anyone.

„He who goes chasing a dragon should be prepared to meet one!" the voice repeated.

He looked up from where the words came and realized that the big trunk he faced, was not a tree but the leg of a huge giant standing right in front of him! This giant was not only very tall but also astonishingly strong, as he crossed his arms over his chest, looking down mockingly at the young fellow trembling like a leaf in the wind.

In shock the miller's son stood paralyzed, his eyes wide open.

„He who goes chasing a dragon should be prepared to meet one", the giant said for a third time.

"I am not afraid of any dragon!", the miller's son argued rebelliously, even though it required all his remaining courage to find words at all.

The giant slowly turned his head, first to one side, then grumbling, to the other side, then again down to the fellow at his feet.

"I do not see anybody here you need to convince."

The miller's son did not know what to reply. So, he came up with a question.

"Who are you, anyway?"

„They call me Odem, the spirit of the forest. I am a distantly related cousin of the Earl of *Consape di Volezza*[2]", the giant replied with great pride.

"You're not a spirit! You're a giant!", the miller's son answered distrustfully.

"As spirit I may appear in any shape I wish. I thought it reasonable in your case to appear as a giant."

Again, the miller's son did not know what to reply.

"Very well", the big creature considered. "You have gotten yourself in quite some trouble here. But no matter what, you deserve a second chance. I will grant you a wish. I will fulfill it, as much as it is in my powers."

"Ha!", the miller's son exclaimed and felt very smart, "I want ten more wishes!"

The giant shook his head, grinning heavily.

"That is a perfect example of what is *not* within my powers."

At that the miller's son finally started thinking. Only one wish! That had to be considered carefully!

Many things came to his mind and swirled around his head, so he did not know which to choose. Being famous and powerful? Many

---

[2] Ital.: consapevolezza = awareness

horses, so he could ride a new one every day? Flying like a bird? Chocolate cake every day? A treasure of gold, so big, he could pay for all other wishes? Maybe a chicken, that would lay golden eggs every day? Maybe even becoming king?

After a while he finally said: "I have to think about it."

"That is a very good decision to start with", the spirit replied. "'May I offer you a seat on my shoulder while doing that? Up here you are safe, and it is an excellent place for thinking."

He reached his big hand down to the young man, so he could climb on it. The giant was taller than any of the trees around him and when he put him on his shoulder, the miller's son could see the treetops underneath like an endless green ocean.

He was surprised to see that up there the sun was still shining, and a clear blue sky stretched widely over to the horizon. Way down in a valley at the other side he could actually see the dragon sleeping. From up there it seemed so small, just like a lap dog. On the hill on the opposite side was the royal castle with its colorful flags on top of the towers and from afar he discovered his father's mill with its slowly turning grind stones. His horse grazed peacefully on the meadow next to it. It had made its way home all by itself.

He also saw the town with its towers and its business and where now all his friends were. A deep sigh escaped from his lungs.

And suddenly he knew what he wanted to wish for.

"I do not want to be alone anymore!", he said. "I want my friends back. Me, being the best of all, being the most courageous of all, being on top of the world is all very nice, but I am all alone up here! Can you bring back my friends? But maybe that is not in your powers? I have withdrawn my friendship from them!"

"That is true", the giant nodded, "but I have not heard them doing the same to you. I will see what I can do. Meanwhile you should sleep a little."

Hardly had the giant spoken these words, the miller's son closed his eyes and fell into a deep sleep.

With only a few steps the giant reached the edge of the forest. Next he put down the lad on a green field. Then he waited for sunset, and when it was finally dark, he went closer to the town, taking care that nobody would see him. He took a deep breath and blew with all his might between the houses and streets, so all the town people believed that a terrible storm had come down. They closed the shutters tightly and pulled their blankets over their heads, waiting for a calmer morning.

The friends of the miller's son, too were afraid of the storm, were thinking with great regret of their friend who they had left all alone out there in the forest.

At the breaking of dawn, the tailor's daughter ran quickly to get her friends to set out searching for him. Together they hurried in big fear that the dragon might have grabbed their friend. But halfway they found him lying in the grass, motionless like dead.

Shocked and speechless, not knowing what to do, they stood around him. It was too late! For a long time, they did not speak.

„It is true, he behaved shamefully, but he still was my dear friend", the blacksmith's son finally said heartbroken.

"He certainly was full of pride and arrogance, but we liked him all the same", the two sons of the town's administrator agreed sadly.

"He had no patience with others and was often unfair, definitely. But deep inside he had a heart", the seamstress' daughter pointed out with distress.

When the miller's son heard these words, his eyes popped open.

In great joy they hugged each other and swore that from now on they would always be there for one another. None of them would ever forget this adventure that had taught them an important lesson.

The six became inseparable friends for life. And if one of them had the slightest sign of a pride attack, the others set him straight immediately!

Four Red Horseshoes

Once upon a time there was a blacksmith, so strong and skillful at his craft that even the royal messengers of the kingdom came to have him forge their horseshoes. His fine craftsmanship was known even across all borders, and knights and chevaliers of many other countries had their swords made by him. He lived alone, was honest, and hardworking and content with his life.

One day a bad storm came over the land and everybody searched for shelter, closing the window shutters and doors of their houses. The blacksmith too put his tools aside to close his workshop. But just as he was about to shut the door firmly, a stranger in a black cape, on a horse as white as snow, passed his house and asked him for refuge. The blacksmith was a kindly natured man, so he showed the horseman where he could put his horse and invited him into his home. After a wholesome meal, the stranger asked him to make a new set of horseshoes for his beautiful horse, still that very night, because he was in a hurry and wanted to set off again, as soon as the storm had calmed down. The blacksmith nodded, re-lit the fire and went back to work.

He hammered and forged the iron into the desired shape. But when he dipped the red glowing metal into the pot with cold water to cool off, the horseshoe remained as red as the fire he had just taken it from! Never before had the blacksmith observed such an incidence and he looked in astonishment, doubting his own eyes.

"That is an attractive color!", the stranger exclaimed. "Precisely as I wanted the horseshoe to look like! You may shoe the horse with it."

The blacksmith did as he was told, and while shoeing the horse with the red horseshoes he continued wondering about this very strange occurrence. But when he had finished and asked for his pay, the stranger mounted his horse and laughed, without even considering taking out his wallet.

The blacksmith, who was a man neither of weak character nor nature, would not stand for it. And since he did not know that the stranger was a wicked wizard, he threatened to take off the horse's shoes again, if the stranger would not pay him a fair price.

The wizard instead became furious, he yelled and shouted and hissed, while his horse was dancing nervously in circles, just like the violent weather outside.

At this very moment, unfortunately, it happened that a young woman with a baby boy in her arms came along the way. She too had been surprised by the storm and was looking for shelter at the blacksmith's house.

When the evil wizard spotted her, he spitefully cursed the poor woman and turned her into a stork, simply because he thought she was the blacksmith's wife. Next, with wicked laughter he whirled around, spurred his horse into a gallop and disappeared into the black night. Only four red shining dots could be made out for a while, until even those dissolved completely into the darkness.

The poor blacksmith - too surprised from the incredible occurrence he had just witnessed - stood there in shock, with a screaming baby at his feet and a stork on the roof.

The day after, however, when the storm had calmed down, he went to town and asked around if anyone knew anything about a missing woman with a child. But nobody was found, not in town nor in the entire country. Finally, he decided to keep the boy and also the stork on the roof, who had already built a nest with the intention to stay as well.

In the following years, the blacksmith raised the child like he was his own son and the stork on the roof of the workshop became the boy's best friend. Every night, before bed time, he would run outside to tell the bird to have "Sweet dreams!" and every night, the stork clattered with its beak, until the boy had gone to sleep.

So it went for many summers, while in winter time the stork flew away with other birds to go south. She always returned the following spring.

Then, one year, the stork did not come back and the nest remained empty. The boy was desperate and since he was not to be comforted about the loss of his dearest friend, the blacksmith decided to come up with a fairy tale. He explained to the boy how the stork had brought him to his house when he was a baby. And while it had always been the duty of these birds to do so, they, of course, could not stay forever. They had to deliver children to other people as well and therefore, one day they needed to go away.

The explanation seemed reasonable enough to the boy and he was no longer sad. Proud of his exciting birth, he started telling everybody in town about it. But people laughed when he did so. And the more he tried to convince them, the more they laughed. This went on and on until he started crying in despair. Only then people would stop laughing and they would pad his head, and nod in assurance.

"Of course! We were just kidding. We believe you. Of course, it was the stork who had delivered you to your father!"

And so the blacksmith's son learnt to cry, whenever he was angry, in order to avoid people mocking him.

Moreover, every time he went outside and looked sadly at the empty nest on the roof, the blacksmith immediately hurried to cheer him up with all sorts of ideas to distract him.

"What is it with these tears on a fine day like this?!", he would say with great laughter, throwing his son up into the air until the boy began to laugh.

And this is how the blacksmith's son learnt to laugh whenever he was sad, to avoid the concerned look on his father's face.

Moreover, every time a big storm came over the land the blacksmith was afraid the wicked wizard might show up again. In order to avoid thinking of it, he took out all the food from the storage, lit all the candles in the house and prepared a great feast, just like he would when celebrating an important holiday.

"What else can one do in such bad weather?!" he used to say and he and his son would sit down and eat and drink for hours.

It was like this that the blacksmith's son learnt to eat whenever he was afraid, in order to keep away the evil thoughts.

Thus, the years went by.

The boy grew into a strong young fellow. He learnt the craftsmanship from his father and eventually forgot all about the stork and the way things were handled around the house to avoid certain situations. Only the ritual of eating whenever there was stormy weather he remembered well.

One day it happened that his father had to go away on important business and a bad storm came up. Anxiously the young lad observed the clouds coming closer until it became almost dark. The wind hurled around the house and the workshop, and the son became very hungry. However, he was all alone and a big feast could not be held in solitude! Therefore, he took his coat and hurried to the tavern in town.

Hardly had he entered the pub, which was crowded with people who had searched shelter from the pouring rain, when he ordered food and drinks for everybody and yelled into the room:

"What else can we do in such bad weather?! Drink and eat, you are my guests!"

It didn't take long for people to order jars full of wine, a variety of dishes, more than the cook could prepare so suddenly, and they laughed and praised the blacksmith's son for his generosity. They even started singing, over and over again:

"What shall we do in such bad weather,
What shall we do in such bad weather,
What shall we do in such bad weather,
Eat and drink all alo-o-ong!"

The tavern's hostess was rubbing her hands with delight, resolutely ordering around her five daughters to fulfill any wish of the guests, until they were not able to swallow one more bite or have one more sip. And since the storm would not calm down quickly, the feast continued until late into the night.

The following morning, very early, someone knocked at the blacksmith's door.

The young fellow opened, still tired and drowsy from all the wine he had drunk the night before. One of the girls from the tavern stood there before him.

"My mother is sending the invoice", she said. "She kindly requests to pay me directly. You might have heard that there have been thieves around and she thinks it's the best for all of us, if the money is in the hands of those it belongs to."

But the sum she asked for was much more than the blacksmith's son had anticipated. He felt ashamed, because he did not know where to find the money. He could not pay the girl and had to send her home without the amount he owed her mother.

She pointed out to him she would get into trouble at home, if she returned with empty hands. However, she gave in, because she knew the blacksmith's son well, trusting his promise he would eventually pay the debt he owed her mother.

With this the young lad began to understand what he had done. His father had always been an honest man and he now had caused him disgrace.

He felt unable to face him again. The dishonour was too big for him to bear. He could not stand this pressure!

So, he stuffed three of his most vital forging tools - a pair of tongs, a hammer and even an anvil - in his back pack, while adding a loaf of bread as well. He also took his warm cloak and hat, and set off.

He did not know which way turn, so he simply followed the road, straight ahead, away from the town where he had grown up and had lived all his life until this day.

He walked for many days and nights, hardly resting, as if his shame was following his footsteps. After climbing a high mountain, he arrived exhausted at the top of a mountain peak. To his big surprise, he noticed a gigantic manor. It was an isolated estate with a wall of big trees and hedges around it, so it was almost impossible to glance inside.

He knocked at the wooden gate and asked for shelter for one night. He was told he could stay in the stable with the horses. He thanked the servant, laid down on the straw and fell immediately asleep.

Around midnight he awoke from the sound of heavy winds, groaning noises and thundering flashes.

Straightaway he became hungry. So hungry, his stomach rumbled so loud that a horse in the back of the stable began to prick up its ears and started pawing with its hooves. The young man took out the remainder of the loaf of bread and was about to take a good bite, when at that very moment his attention was drawn to a curious detail.

He stepped closer to have a better look.

The horse's shoes were red as fire!

Right then, he understood instantaneously! These were the four red horseshoes his father had forged and never had received his fair pay for!

His shock about this discovery was so big that he let the bread drop to the ground, because he understood he was in the house of the wicked wizard. The horse immediately grabbed the bread and swallowed it.

Again, the animal pawed noisily with its hooves.

The blacksmith's son did not hesitate a moment.

He grabbed an apple he had picked off a tree along the way and calmed the animal with this unexpected tasty snack. Then he took out his tools and started to take off the horseshoes, one by one. He knew the procedure well enough he could have done it with his eyes closed.

But not with a stomach pinching him in such a way! Over and over again he had to interrupt his work and was writhing in pain, holding his tummy. But he continued his task nevertheless.

Hardly had he removed the first horseshoe, it burst into rusty pieces and trickled down onto the floor like sand. The same happened with the second horseshoe. The third and the last one, however, kept their shape. He quickly put them into his bag, wanting to leave this creepy place as soon as possible.

But the moment he stepped outside he heard the clattering of beaks of a stork above his head and when he looked up, he saw hundreds of birds sitting on top of the roof. All of them were tied to a pole by means of a long chain and they looked down sadly on him.

He hesitated, because back in the stable the horse began to be very upset about the loss of the four red horseshoes. The animal began to make such noise, that surely the evil wizard would soon take notice of it.

But the son could not bear the sight of the poor birds and so he climbed on the roof, took out the heavy pliers of his bag and cut the chain. One stork after the other spread its wings and flew away into the dark sky.

Now he needed to leave this creepy place in a hurry!

But when he returned to the spot where he had put the ladder, it was no longer there. It had slipped and fallen when he had taken the last step up and the roof was way too high to jump down.

Now he could have done with some good advice!

If the wizard awoke and discovered him on the roof, he would be lost!

He did not want to despair, but he had to admit to himself that his situation was a "lose-lose" one. Either he killed himself jumping down, or the evil wizard would curse him, to think the least. In any case he would never see his father again, who he had left in shame!

With this thought tears began to run down his cheeks. Since there was no one distracting him with other thoughts, they started flowing like a creek, then like a river, then like a stream. The storm had calmed down, but now the entire roof was wet with tears. He was so caught up in his despair that he did not notice how some beaks softly pulled at his clothes.

When he finally looked up, he found himself surrounded by storks who each held an end of his shirt in its beaks and softly pulled him up into the air with flapping wings. They carried him silently through the black night, through the air, into the darkness far away. Floating softly on countless wings in such a way, the young lad believed to be dreaming. He almost thought to be a bird himself!

The storks were flapping heavily with their wings and to make it easier for them, the blacksmith's son reached into his bag to take out the remaining two horseshoes, that had not dissolved into sand and that he had taken with him.

He let go of the third one, weighing as heavy as lead. Already the load seemed to have lessened to a great extent. But when he took out the fourth horseshoe, pure gold was dazzling before his eyes. It was so pure, that even the scarce light of the stars was enough to make it shine.

What a marvelous surprise this was! He laughed with joy about the unexpected fortune. Now he could pay back to his father the debt he had caused him, and even more!

When the sun was rising on the horizon, he spotted his home town from afar. He saw the king's castle with its familiar flags on top of the hill. He recognized the big wind wheel of the miller's place and finally, he made out his father's workshop.

There the birds softly put him down on the grass and rested for a moment before taking off again. The lad got drowsily up to his feet, straightened his clothes and waved them good bye.

During all this time the poor blacksmith had been sick with worry about his lost son and when he saw him arriving at his workshop, he ran outside with open arms to welcome him with great joy. Father and son hugged and laughed, and laughed and hugged.

The blacksmith listened to the story of his son with eyes big of astonishment when he reported to him how, with great courage, he had taken the four red horseshoes off the wizard's horse.

From that day on they no longer held great feasts in order to keep away the evil during a storm. And the young lad cried whenever he was sad, and he laughed whenever he felt joy, and he showed anger, whenever he felt angry.

With the gold of the last horseshoe not only the bill of the tavern was settled. Both, father and son, enjoyed a good income for a long time after.

During the following summers many storks arrived in town and built nests on the chimneys of the houses and on top of the roofs and the rattling of their beaks was heard all over the land.

The people, however, had seen with their very own eyes, how the blacksmith's son had been brought back to his house by the storks. From that day on they themselves told everybody the incredible story, whether they wanted to hear it or not, over and over again!

The King's Messenger

Once upon a time there was a young man who was considered the fastest in the whole kingdom. Since he was the son of the Royal Cook he had grown up at court and had had the pleasure of playing with the other children there. His father had wanted to teach him his craftsmanship, but the child had not wanted to hear about it. As soon as he had seen an opportunity, he had escaped to run outside over the fields and practise his skill.

He had always been an exceptionally good runner and more than anything he had enjoyed racing with the other children. No matter how often they had tried, they had never been able to beat him. Until one day, when the young daughter of the horse keeper caught up with him. What a terrible experience this had been for him! But to make things worse, she continued doing so every time they had raced after that. This had upset him very much and continued bothering him, as he had not been able to overcome this feeling of defeat inside, no matter how much time had gone by. Thus, he had grown into an obsessed, eager young man, who put all his energy into only one goal: winning.

One day the royal couple searched for a new messenger. The courier should be fast and trustworthy. The Queen and the King had heard of the two youngsters at their court and since they could not decide between the girl and the lad, they simply called both to be their personal messengers.

From then on, they could use all the king's horses that were spread throughout the country at a day's ride. Thus, a messenger would always find a fresh horse enabling him to continue his journey without delay.

The cook's son was very proud of his new position and tried to demonstrate to the world that he was the better messenger. He never missed a chance to do so and granted himself no rest. But, in spite of his endeavours, the royal couple continued to treat him and the young woman with equal appreciation and would give assignments one day to her, the other to him. So, both rode through wind, rain and snow, from one end of the country to the other, and whenever they passed people in their elegant royal messenger's uniform, folks gazed at them in admiration. They, too, would not make any distinction between the female and the male messenger. So, it went on and the young man became more and more agitated about his fruitless attempts to finally beat the female messenger.

One day the royal couple called both of them to court to assign them a very important secret task.

"It is about time that the young Prince marries", they said. "This is a secret matter; nobody should know about it yet. And since he is not very fond of girls, we need to find another young gentleman. So, go and collect pictures of any fine man that has the same characteristics and interests as our son. We need to find an exceptional match. Please be quick and bring us what you can find."

Both messengers bowed and hurried immediately to their horses. Never before had they gone on such an important assignment! Without exchanging one word they rode off, each in the opposite direction. This time, the young man thought to himself that he would perform better than she!

After only a short distance riding like the wind, the young man noticed from afar a small person standing at the side of the road. When he came closer, he saw that it was a young child. He brought his horse to a halt and looked in astonishment down to the deserted child who looked at him with big eyes filled with hope.

He sat up again in his saddle and looked around, but he could not see anybody. The little child seemed to be all alone. The matter did arouse his curiosity; a young child should not be on a dangerous road alone like this, he thought for a moment. But then he remembered his duty and felt that he could not afford to lose any time. He grabbed an apple out of his bag and handed it to the child.

"Go home to your mother!", he spoke, "you will become sick if you sit here like this!"

And with these words he spurred his horse on and rode off. Too many kingdoms waited for him to arrive and he simply had no time to take care of other things.

Many weeks and months passed. He travelled from one country to another and from each he collected pictures of fine young men who had something special about them. But eventually this task turned into a more difficult one than he had expected, because the Queen and the King had not specified what special characteristics they were looking for. And there were so many in this world! One candidate was very intelligent, the next extraordinarily handsome. Others were unfortunate in size or nature, but equally special. Others again could tell of ill-fated stories or proved to be gifted with outstanding talents, in any case exceptional. The list of fine young men with something unique about them became longer and longer, until he got so confused that he did no longer know what to look for.

He strove to collect miniature paintings of at least one candidate of every unique trait. The more he rushed, the farther away he seemed to get from the castle. Soon he had so many pictures in his bag that he needed to exchange some of them to have space for new ones. Every time he sat long hours gazing at his collection, not knowing which painting to eliminate. No matter how far he travelled, how fast he moved, how many pictures he collected, or how hard he tried, he felt he could never fulfill his task.

Three times the leaves of the trees had fallen. Three times snow and ice had covered the road. Three times spring had come with fresh grass and flowers along the way. At the fourth time of summer he finally decided to make his way back to the castle, even though in his heart he felt dissatisfied and weary.

When he reached the road at almost half a day's ride to the castle, he could not believe his eyes! Again, from afar, he noticed the little child sitting at the side of the road. He approached slowly and, like at the first encounter, he reined in his horse.

The child looked at him with big eyes filled with hope.

"Why are you still sitting there?!", he asked even more astonished than the first time.

Again, the child did not answer.

He grabbed a sweet cake that he had bought as a specialty from another country. He broke it into two pieces and handed one part to the child.

"Go home to your father!", he spoke. "You cannot stay here. It is dangerous for a child to be alone out here on the road!"

And, as he had done on the first occasion, he spurred his horse on and continued on his way. He had to rush back to the castle to finally deliver his collection of possible suitors to the Queen and the king. They had been waiting far too long for his return. He had no more time to waste!

But when his horse raced into the courtyard, he discovered the girl's horse already at rest at the stable. And when he rushed to the royal hall to present his collection of pictures, he found the Queen and the King sitting in admiration in front of a row of portraits.

They thanked him all the same and handed him a golden coin with the emblem of the crown. But the coin would not give him much pleasure, because he grieved the fact of arriving second again.

Grumbling, he returned to his horse and without granting it the well-deserved rest, he raced out the castle's gate in such a fury, that all chickens, geese, cats and dogs scattered in all directions, cackling, barking, hissing and chattering. It was quite a spectacle. All the servants in the castle looked up startled, shaking their heads, as they watched him disappear into the fields.

The young fellow sprinted across the countryside without paying any attention to where he was going. He crossed meadows and creeks and bushes, and only when he got close to the big forest, he finally slowed down a little. He reined in his horse, turned around in his saddle and, for the first time, looked back to where he had come from. He peered into the distance but could not recognize anything anymore. No familiar sights, no people, no villages and not even the castle on the top of the hill. There was nothing there anymore. Moreover, the countryside around him seemed strange and unfamiliar.

Slowly he turned his horse around and led it back the way he had come. But the farther he went, the more unusual the surroundings became. He made the horse trot, hoping to discover something recognizable farther down the road. He looked to the left and searched to the right, turning around again and again, but nothing seemed to be familiar anymore.

How could this have happened? He was such an experienced messenger and now he had lost his way!

Once again, he made his horse turn around and gallop back on the road as fast as the miserable beast was able to run. But it led to no other result than to exhaust the poor animal. He still found himself in a totally strange setting. He felt confused and did not know what to do anymore.

At this very moment he remembered the little child on the side of the road. In this strange and creepy situation, the child seemed to be the only familiar reference. He went back to see if he could find somebody to help him with directions, hoping to recognize a human being anywhere near.

The child was still sitting there in silence, and, more than that, it seemed almost to be waiting for him. As soon as he got off his horse, the child raised itself, and took his hand without a word.

He let it happen and thought that surely it must have some home nearby and that its parents would be able to tell him the way back.

He followed the child into the forest, holding its hand, through bushes and trees. At a clearing the little child stopped, pointing with his hand to a tiny dilapidated house with draughty windows.

"Can you fix this for me?", the child spoke for the first time and again looked at the messenger with eyes filled with hope.

"How about that!? Finally! You are able to speak!", the young man marveled. "Why have you never replied to me before?"

"Oh, I did, I did!", the child answered. "But you would not hear me. Will you fix my house for me?"

The young man approached the small building and looked at it more closely. It certainly needed a fixing job! It was in poor condition. With a little tender loving care, however, it could be turned into a cozy little home again, he thought.

"Over there is wood!" The child showed him a pile of wood.

"And here is a saw!" It pointed to a toolbox next to it.

"And here is a slicer!", the child added, as the young man followed silently its instructions and handed him the device.

Hesitantly the royal messenger took the saw. What an awkward request from an even more awkward child that was!

Still baffled by it all, he eventually began to work. He thought he might as well help the child a little, while he was waiting for someone to come along. Maybe his rival, the girl messenger, would come by and he could secretly follow her back to the castle without having to admit that he had lost his way?

Within a short time, he had measured and cut some boards and soon he hung his messenger's uniform on the branch of a tree, because he had become hot. The child happily jumped around him and showed him exactly where to place the boards. The young man attached and nailed one after the other and soon the tiny house looked much better.

When he got hungry, he sat down and shared his food with the child. They sat side by side on a chopped tree trunk, ate quietly and the young man thought, that never before his food had tasted that delicious!

When they had finished eating, the little child stretched out in the grass in the sun, reached out to take his hand and said: "We shall rest a little! Join me!"

And again, the royal messenger thought that never before the warmth of the sun had felt so enjoyable to him!

After a while the young man returned to work with fresh energy and when it got dark, the repair of the tiny house was finished. The child stood in front of it with glowing cheeks and brilliant eyes.

"It is marvelous!", it exclaimed and clapped its hands for joy, "Never before has my house been so beautiful! I am very grateful to you!"

The child turned around and handed a rose to his new friend, who accepted the flower that was nothing more than a fragile bud that immediately pricked his finger. For a moment the child started to laugh but then became very serious and explained to the messenger:

"You need to give this rose to the right person! Do you understand? Otherwise it will live for only three days and after that, it will die and with it, my house will collapse again. Will you please take care of this?"

Again, the messenger was more than confused.

"But how can I know who the right person is?", he asked.

"How am I supposed to know?", the child answered, as if this question had been the most unusual question of all questions in the world. "Only you can know that! Promise me that you will take care of this?"

The child looked at him with such expectation that the young man gave in and promised to do what the boy had requested.

When he nodded his head, the child turned around satisfied and crawled into the tiny house.

"I will lay down to sleep now", it explained. "'You are too big to come in. But you may rest here in front of my door on the moss. Sweet dreams!"

So, the royal messenger rolled out the horse blanket to sleep in front of the tiny house. He was so tired from the day's work that he soon fell asleep and did not wake up until the next morning.

When the sun tickled his nose, he stretched and yawned and thought that never before he had slept so well! How quiet and peaceful the morning was!

He jumped onto his feet and rolled up the blanket.

Then he stepped to the door in front of which he had slept and knocked softly, trying to wake the child.

But there was no answer.

He knocked a little louder, but still there was no answer.

And when he knocked the third time, this time with strength and loud enough to be heard from afar, the tiny house vanished into a fog right in front of his eyes. He tried to seize the wall he had fixed the day before, but when he did, his hand only touched air.

He rubbed his eyes in disbelieve.

Where there had been solid wood just a moment earlier, now there was nothing but air! He closed his eyes and opened them again, three times, but the tiny house was gone and together with it, the child. Only the rose with its fragile bud lay there where the house had been.

Carefully the young man wrapped the flower into a damp cloth and placed it into one of the saddle bags, with only the rose bud peeking out. He took one last look, hoping to find the child again, but he remained all alone in the silence of the forest.

Taking a deep breath and with the determination to find his way back somehow, he mounted his horse. When he was back in the saddle again, he suddenly could see the towers of the castle on the hill at the horizon and he wondered why he had not seen them the day before?

Slowly he guided his horse back onto the road that led towards the rising sun and he was very thoughtful. Never before had he moved so leisurely.

When he arrived at the castle's gate the girl messenger riding her horse passed him on her way out.

"What a beautiful rose!", she immediately exclaimed stopping her horse next to him.

The young man looked down at the flower. He had forgotten all about it, while trying to figure out the sudden disappearance of the child. Now the rose bud had opened giving off a marvelous sent.

"I have to water the rose!", he replied remembering his promise as he turned away and spurring on his horse to enter the castle's courtyard. Then he attached a little drinking bottle to his belt so he could carry the rose with him at all times.

The next day the girl messenger passed him again in the castle's garden and, once more, exclaimed in great admiration: "What a wonderful perfume!"

The messenger looked down at his belt and noticed that the flower already appeared less fresh than the day before. He had not yet figured out how to keep his promise and it scared him. So, again, he hurried to exchange the water without paying attention to the girl. For this reason, the flower lost one petal that night.

The third day the girl messenger brought a jug of fresh water to the young man.

"This is for your rose!", she said. "I wish your flower to live as long as possible!"

The young man assured her that there was no need, because he himself had just exchanged the water. That night, the rose lost all its leaves and the young messenger became desperate.

He remembered the words of the child well that he had to give the flower to the right person. So, he rushed in despair to the royal couple to give the rose to them. Surely a Queen and a King were the right persons to give the flower to!

But the Queen looked at him with astonishment.

"Why would you give us a dying flower without any petals?", she asked.

And, indeed, he had to admit that the rose was in an even sadder condition than before. Only then he began to understand that the one person to recognize the beauty of this flower had been the girl messenger. Only she could save the flower's life!

"She is on an assignment in a town in our kingdom", the Queen explained. "But if you hurry, you may be able to catch up with her."

There was no time to be lost!

He turned around, grabbed a rested horse and raced off immediately, faster than he had ever done. He kept the rose underneath his jacket and with every move he made it sting him into his heart.

Already the sun was settling down behind the trees, when he finally spotted the girl far off in the distance, almost at the horizon. However, by now she seemed to be on her way back to the castle.

When they approached each other, she recognized him waving her hand. Their horses met and stopped, and the young man handed over the rose to her.

When the girl touched it, the flower opened and immediately produced a strong fragrance. Roots started growing from its stem and looped around both their hands, so it was impossible to separate them again. They looked at each other and understood that they were meant to be together.

Side by side they slowly rode back to the castle and told everybody the happy news. They even exchanged horses and promised to never race again.

From that day on they shared any duty. Now it was his turn, the next it was hers. And sometimes it happened that they even went together.

They settled in a nice little home and planted the rose in front of it. Soon it grew into a rose bush that covered the entire roof in blossoms and encircled their home in an everlasting cloud of heavenly perfume. And sometimes at night, when it was very peaceful, the king's messenger could hear a child laughing from afar.

Three Pearls

A long time ago, before people had discovered the golden treasure of honey for sweetening their dishes, there had been a huge apple tree in the centre of a kingdom that was so tall, that its branches reached high into the sky and its trunk was so boundless that three men had to hold hands in order to surround it.

One day a farmer bought the land, on which the tree rooted. Since it had been many years that the tree had beard fruits, he decided to cut it down to create a field for grain instead.

But the farmer did not know that the trunk was almost hollow inside. This space had given secure shelter for a Queen bee with her

140

colony. Every day the bees started out from this safe place to collect nectar from all the apple trees in the kingdom to make their honey.

When the farmer cut down the tree with only a few chops, the entire bee colony was shaken up and fell apart in thousand pieces. Upset and confused the bees hurried out to see what the cause of this "earth quake" was, and when they discovered the farmer, they all united to attack him and chase him away.

The poor man threw away his ax and ran off screaming and hollering in pain, holding his hands to his bottom, because the bees had stung him there many times.

He found refuge in a creek nearby, plunged right in and did not come out again, until the insects had given up their pursuit.

Meanwhile the outraged Queen bee was looking at her destroyed house. She addressed her colony: "We do not have a house anymore. Now, each one of you has to find shelter on your own, until we will have constructed a new home. Beware of these humans! They are evil! They do not respect us nor our existence. That is why, from now on, you will sting them where ever you can. Now, re-building our home has priority! Do not collect any nectar, until we will have finished this task!"

That is why during the following summer all people got stung by bees as never before. Children were afraid to play outside, and farmers could hardly work their fields without being chased by swarms of insects. Even in the town people could not open a window without being harassed. Life became very tiresome.

But it did get even worse.

In autumn, when the crops should be harvested in the entire kingdom there was not one apple to be picked. People stood in front of the empty trees, scratching their heads, wondering what the cause of this total loss was.

Some thought it was the wicked work of witches. Others even believed burglars from a foreign kingdom had secretly come to take away all the fruits. And many were simply afraid, because they were convinced that malicious spirits had brought this evil over them. But nobody had any advice as to what to do.

The Queen and the King send out their best women and men to find out what the reason was. But winter came, their people had no fruits to eat and they still had no clue what the cause of this problem was.

The farmer, who had cut the tree, was still in bed, because the bees had stung him the most of all the people. As soon as he had dared to leave the house, big swarms of bees had attacked him once again. He was injured with so many stings that not even his own wife recognized his swollen face anymore.

That was why he sent his youngest son to prepare the field for the spring time and to finally dig out the big roots of the chopped apple tree.

When the young farmer's son started excavating the earth, he saw a single bee sitting tired in the bark. It was an old bee that could no longer fly and had had to stay behind, when all her fellow bees had left.

Carefully the young lad took her in his hand and put her down on the side in a protected area.

But to his great surprise he heard the bee speak to him:

"Do not worry! I am old and cannot do you any harm anymore. All the other bees have gone away. Our Queen is very angry, because you have destroyed our house. Until your species will make peace with my species there will be no more apples! Our Queen has forbidden us to collect nectar from the blossoms of the apple trees."

"So that is the reason for this problem!", the farmer's son exclaimed. But then he shrugged his shoulders saying: "But what can I do about it? I am only a poor farmer's son."

„Go and find the shell with the three pearls and bring them to the Earl *Consape di Volezza*[3]. Only he will understand the message and tell you the secret solution!"

"Who is this Earl? I have never heard of him. And where do I find this shell?", the lad asked.

"All I can tell you is that he is very rarely seen. He is the noble ghost of the royal castle. But where you will find the shell, I really don't know. You have to figure that out yourself. But do not wait too long! Time is precious!"

---

[3] Ital: Consapevolezza: awareness

And with this the old bee crawled behind a piece of wood and went to sleep.

The farmer's son set out right away, without even telling anybody. He knew a fisherman who lived on the shore of the ocean at a one day's walking distance. Surely, he would know a lot about the sea and fish and shells, and he would be the right fellow to ask.

"You can work and fish with me every day", the fisher suggested. "Maybe you will find what you are looking for"

From then on, every morning before dawn the farmer's son set sail with the fisherman and later in the day, they sold what they had caught at the fish market. He checked every shell for the three pearls before selling it.

So, it went day after day, week after week, but not a single pearl was ever found. Nonetheless, the young farmer persisted and would not give up easily. Spring time passed into summer, summer into fall and soon winter announced its turn with its first icy winds.

One of these days a poor man in torn rags came to the market and asked for some left-over fish, so he could cook a soup for himself and his family. The fisherman sent him away, saying: "We only sell excellent quality fish. We have no leftovers."

But the farmer's son had a good heart and gave the man his own fish, that he had taken aside for his dinner.

"I have no money to pay you", the pitiable man said. "But I will give you this shell. It only opens to those who have a pure heart."

The man handed him a shell and when the farmer's son held it in his hands, it very slowly opened.

Amazed the young man observed the movement of the shell in his hand.

"The shell with the three pearls!", he exclaimed in great exaltation, when he discovered three shiny round little beads inside.

He wanted to thank the poor man, but when he looked up, he had already disappeared.

The farmer's son carefully packed the shell with the pearls in his bag, thanked his friend the fisherman and set out to go to the castle to find the Earl *Consape di Volezza*, as the bee had told him.

After three days of wandering he arrived at the castle.

Immediately he asked the castle's administrator if he had any work for him. That way he hoped to be able to stay in the castle and look for the Earl.

But the administrator shook his head. All positions in the castle were taken. There was absolutely no need for another worker.

"You can try your luck in town tomorrow morning", the administrator suggested. "For tonight you may sleep in the barn with the horses."

The farmer's son thanked the castle's administrator and prepared his bed in the hay near by the horses. But he had set his mind on finding the Earl. So, instead of going to town, as the administrator suggested, he decided to ask for a personal appointment with the royal couple and ask them directly for this

Earl. With this thought he fell asleep and soon he had a vivid dream, because he was very tired from the long journey.

"I hear you have come to see me?", suddenly a voice directly next to him said.

A fairly short man stood there, right in front of his bed of hay, cleaning the dust off his clothes and then majestically raising his head. He was quite pale, almost transparent, but had a kind smile.

"I am looking for the Earl *Consape di Volezza*", answered the farmer's son straight out.

"He is standing right in front of you. I am the castle's ghost you are looking for", the little man answered. "The old bee already has told me that you would come. Did you find the shell?"

The young fellow handed him the open shell with the three pearls.

The Earl took it and investigated them closely and from all sides.

"Indeed", he mumbled, more to himself than to the farmer's son, "it's them! It has been quite a while that I have seen them."

He took one pearl between his fingers and rubbed it.

Fine sand trickled from his fingers onto the floor, where it created a little heap, that subsequently turned into a piece of wood. He looked at the object and nodded in satisfaction.

Then he grabbed the second pearl and rubbed it between his fingers.

This time the sand turned into a role of paper, on which was written in large letters: "King's announcement".

Again, the little man nodded very pleased.

However, when he rubbed the third pearl, the sand dissolved into air as soon as it touched ground. And when the last grain of sand was gone, the little man faded away as well, as if he was part of the process.

Early next morning the rooster called everybody to work, before the sun had even started to rise. The farmer's son rubbed his eyes, still sleepy, and thought about the strange dream he had had that night.

But, alas, when he wanted to grab the shell, he had put right next to his hay pillow, it was no longer there. Instead there was a piece of wood and a paper roll.

Ruminating what this was all about, he turned both objects in his hands. He just could not figure it out! What was the significance of this? Where had the pearls gone? Did someone steal them from him while he had been sleeping? Here, in the royal castle!? He did not want to believe that. Had it been a dream or had the Earl visited him in reality?

He tried to remember his dream, but it would not come back clearly. If it had been the Earl, who had left him these items, then why a piece of wood and a paper roll?

At that moment he discovered words on the roll of paper and read aloud in astonishment: "Royal Announcement".

At these words a firm voice behind his back made him jump in surprise.

"What are you doing?"

He looked right into the eyes of the young Princess.

He had never seen her in person, had only heard people telling stories about the extraordinary intelligence of her and her brother.

He did not know, what to reply, but he was sure that she had to be the prettiest girl he had ever seen.

The Princess had come to the barn because she had wanted to ride her horse before breakfast at sunrise. When she saw this lad bent over, totally absorbed in something, she had become curious.

"What is it you are holding in your hands?", she asked nosily.

"It seems to be the solution to the missing apples in the kingdom", the farmer's son answered honestly, surprising himself with that reply, because the thought had only crossed his mind the moment he spoke. "But I cannot understand the significance of it."

And then he told the Princess the whole story about the old bee and how he had started searching for the three pearls. She sat down next to him on a bale of straw and listened with great interest.

"But isn't it obvious?", she exclaimed at the end of his tale. "We humans have stolen security from the bee colony! Well, one of us has: your father. But to bees, this is all the same. Now they believe all humans will always destroy their homes."

"You are right!", the farmer's son agreed much impressed by her remark.

"And we do not value their work, because we do not understand. And that is why they are stinging us!", she continued, reflecting out loud. "But now we know better! We know that this is not true! They are very important to us humans!"

„You are indeed as smart as people say!", the young man said in even bigger admiration.

"Not worth mentioning", the girl answered. "You are brave! I would not have dared to go out into the world, all the way to the ocean, to look for the pearls."

"I know what I can do!"

Again, the farmer's son spoke out loud another thought that crossed his mind at this very moment. "I will build a new house for the bees out of this piece of wood! A much fancier one than they had before!"

"What an excellent idea!", the Princess agreed and grabbed the roll of paper. "And this may be a task just suited for me! Look! There is written 'King's Announcement'!"

She pointed with her finger to the letters on the paper.

"I will speak with my parents. They can announce to the whole kingdom that bee houses shall be protected from now on. And they can inform all the people of the valuable work the bees are doing for us in making the apples grow. And then, people will cherish them forever!"

"Again, you are right!", the farmer's son nodded impressed. "This is the significance of the second pearl. But what about the third one? There is no hint?"

The two young people looked at each other and shrugged their shoulders.

"Let's not get desperate", the Princess suggested. "What good is it to worry about the third task, if we still have not fulfilled the first two? Let's get this done and then we will see about it."

The farmer's son was allowed to work in the castle's carpentry shop. After only three days the new bee house was finished. Together with the Princess the farmer's son set out to install the house near the edge of the forest, were there was also a little creek with clear water. At the same time the news about the precious work of the bees was announced over the whole country.

A couple of days later the Princess and the farmer's son went back to the place to see if the Queen bee had accepted the place and had moved in with her population. They were more than overjoyed to see that there was a busy coming and going at the new hive.

Contentedly they shook hands.

Now, everything would turn out for the better.

Just as they wanted to turn around and go back, a familiar voice spoke to the farmer's son.

"The Queen gives her thanks to you."

The old bee had hardly been able to get up, taken utmost care not to be accidently stepped upon.

"You have given us back our self-esteem!", the old bee explained.

"What do you mean by that?", the farmer's son wondered.

"Well, I will explain it to you", continued the insect. "You have built us a new home. With that, you have given back our security. You have taken care that everybody now is informed about our work and that humans respect us for it. Security and respect are good nourishment for self-esteem."

The young lad's face became thoughtful trying to understand these words.

"All living creatures need these three basics", she continued. "Didn't you know that?"

"The third pearl!", the farmer's son exclaimed snipping his fingers, because suddenly he understood the whole story.

"Exactly", the bee nodded. "And because of that you shall have a little jar of honey every year."

"Honey?", the young man asked again wondering. He felt stupid, because this little insect kept talking about things he had never heard of.

"Stick in your finger and taste it!", she suggested and showed him a small, jar like honeycomb, filled with a golden liquid.

And how marvelous it tasted!

"Do come back every year and we will fill this little jar for you."

The farmer's son took the little pot, thanked the bee and made his way back home, very happy.

His father was angry with him, because he had not prepared the field as he had been told. But when he tasted the honey and heard the whole story, he gave in and was simply glad about the return of his son.

The year after all trees in the entire kingdom carried more fruits than ever, and they were sweeter than ever before. And when the time had come the young man received his promised jar of honey.

Soon the message spread that for a few coins one could buy a little of this valuable golden liquid from the farmer.

As the offspring of the Queen of bees grew up and multiplied, the farmer's son built another home for them as well. In return he got another pot of honey, more than his family could eat and soon he had a good income from this sweet treasure.

Every year the farmer's son sent a little cup of honey to the Princess and over time, they became dear friends.

From that time on people treated bees only with the greatest respect.

And if it occurred that someone was stung by a bee, everybody knew it must have been an unfortunate misunderstanding.

The Bear's Treasure

Once upon a time, there was a young Princess who lived in a castle built on top of a hill. She and her brother had been taught everything a young Princess and Prince needed to know. Being the eldest, it didn't take the diligent and obedient Princess long to know the most important things a Princess needed to know.

However, when the Princess grew into a young woman, she gradually began to get bored. Each day was like the other, always filled with the same things. In the morning she had to get dressed and had her hair brushed thoroughly. Then she had to listen to the lectures of her teachers, who for quite some time did not have anything new to tell her.

In the afternoon she had to sit with the ladies and embroider delicate fabrics, even though she already had a fine collection of these embroideries. In the evening she had to get undressed, and, once again had her hair brushed until she went to bed.

That is how it went day after day, week after week, month after month and she became very tired of her life. So, one day, she decided to look for a duty worthy of a Princess.

She asked one of the ladies if she didn't know anything more sophisticated, she could help with. Immediately the lady in waiting brought in an enormous piece of fabric that was to be embroidered, which would take years to complete.

She said: "This is a beautiful task for a Princess! Never before has a royal highness embroidered such a huge cloth."

Instantaneously the Princess put herself to work. In the afternoon she now cross-stitched the big cloth instead of embroidering the small pieces. But soon enough she noticed that it was more of the same and she became bored again.

She asked the Royal Cook if he would know of any duty he could assign to her? Something no other Princess had ever done before.

The cook shook his head.

"If I delegate these duties to you, what then should the maids and the servants do? I would have to send them home and they no longer would have an income. That is just not right!"

After that she asked the keeper of the royal horses, who was a very clever man. He did not want to get into trouble, so he answered in a very diplomatic way.

"I am afraid, here in the stable there is not much to do. The royal horses are well-trained, there's little work. But exercising them regularly, riding them on a daily basis, would be quite helpful. This seems to be a duty suitable for a Princess, because that way you will also get to know the people in the kingdom."

"What a wonderful idea! I will do that!", the young Princess exclaimed.

From that day on she could be seen riding across the fields, rain or shine, through forests and villages, waving at the people in the countryside. She was more than happy about this very important task, because whenever she passed people they would wave back, cheer and smile at her, and even bow in front of her. They truly seemed to appreciate what she was doing.

But soon she started to become bored of even that as well.

Then it happened one day when she was passing the river, that she observed a young man standing on a rock in the middle of the strong current. In his hands he was holding a fishing rod and next to him there was a basket filled with fish. He obviously was in danger, because a big bear wanting to check out the delicious fish in the hamper, was slowly approaching him. The young man was fiercely waving his arms and the rod and was yelling at the bear to leave him alone. But the bear was not to be chased away. Instead, it rose up to its full height, twice as tall as the young man and roared ferociously. One blow with its paw would be enough to kill the poor fellow! Only she could save him, the Princess thought!

Shortly before, the Princess had bought a jar of honey from a farmer. Quickly she led her horse to a safe spot a little away from the river and put down the opened jar within sight and smell of the bear.

And, sure enough, the sweet scent of the honey made the beast's head turn in the direction of the pot of honey. The animal approached the honey and let go of the idea to get the fish. While the bear was licking the golden syrup, the Princess quietly led her horse to the young man, telling him to sit behind her saddle and off they went.

He was one of the sons of the city mayor, a handsome young lad, whom she had observed before at official balls. And since he was very grateful to the Princess for saving his life, they promised each other to meet again at the same spot the same time the following day. And, they met again the day after, and the day after that, until they fell in love. Soon after they got married, and the young man moved into the castle, where the couple were given a room in one of the towers.

From that day on they went fishing together. He stood on the rock in the middle of the current, fishing, while she made sure that nothing bad would happen, keeping an eye on the surrounding area. In the evening they would bring a basket full of fish to the castle. The Princess could not remember happier days than these.

After a while the people in the castle became tired of eating the fish the couple brought home every day. The cook served nothing else day after day. Even the Queen and the King did not want to eat it anymore. So, one day they said to their daughter: "Take a break! It's too much fish!"

Therefore, the young husband decided to go hunting instead,

and his young wife accompanied him making sure they were safe, because an evil dragon dwelled in the forest and everybody knew how dangerous it was to go there. Every morning they went out, hunted all day long and in the evening, they brought back fresh meat. Again, the Princess could not remember happier days than these.

But after some time, the game keeper came to the Queen and the King to report that too much hunting was causing a serious decline in the wild game population.

From then on the young husband started passing his days like a Prince. In the morning he got dressed and had his beard done. Then he listened to the stories of the royal jester. But his tales did not turn out to be a good enough substitute for the excitement the young man had lost. In the afternoon he went out with other noble men to practice the crossbow. In the evening, he got undressed and had his beard done, until he went to bed with his wife.

That's how life went by, day after day, week after week and month after month, and gradually the Princess became increasingly tired of her husband. There was no more need to watch out for him to keep him safe. She became more and more grumpy. In her opinion, nobody in the castle could do anything right anymore, least of all her husband. Servants tried to stay out of her way. And so did her husband.

She became very unhappy with him and blamed him for no longer being the fabulous man she had once married. And since he felt the same way about her, one day he finally took his fishing rod, saddled his horse and left.

Upon receiving this news, the Princess moaned bitterly. She wept day and night and the flow of her tears would not dry up. But no matter how much she cried, her husband did not return.

During one of these dreadful nights a frightening dream came over her. She dreamt that a ghost spoke to her: "Go and find the bear! Ask it what to do. Only the bear knows the answer to your problem."

She was so upset about the dream, that the next morning she immediately went to the river, put down a jar of honey and waited for the bear. It was not for long for the bear to show up, slowly trotting along, as if it had expected her.

The Princess was scared, because this time she was not sitting on the horse at a safe distance. She gathered all her courage and spoke to the bear: "My dearest bear! My husband has left me. I do want him to come back and again be the exciting man he once was. Can you help me?"

"Why should I do that?", the bear replied calmly, having a taste of the honey. "There is enough I have to deal with every day. I don't have time to worry about the problems of all the Princesses in this world."

"I will give you something in return", the Princess said. "I will leave you a jar of honey or a basket of fish every day, in return for your help."

The bear grumbled grudgingly, turned around and trotted away saying no more.

The Princess stood speechless. What unappreciative behaviour! He had finished all the honey and now went away without giving anything in return. She certainly would not accept that! But since the beast did not show any consideration, she had no other choice but to get up and follow him.

She straggled behind the bear along the river, over the hills and the fields, until they reached the forest. Without her horse, just walking, she feared the dragon. But the bear went on without even looking back at her and the Princess had no choice but to follow him again.

On it went over roots and rocks, through bristles and bushes, with her dress constantly getting caught in thorny shrubs. She had to pull and tear it to move ahead. Before long the dress turned into a dirty rag covering her body. Finally, the bear, without looking back, stopped and crawled into a cave.

Again, the Princess hesitated; she did not know what to do. Already the night had begun to fall and it started getting cold and dark. She was afraid to follow the beast into his cave. But in the end, again, she did not have any other choice in order to get what she wanted. Moreover, if she wanted to avoid the dragon, she would have to go inside.

Cautiously she crawled through the black hole.

Inside the Princess gazed with wide open eyes, as she found the bear lying in a warm nest with three little cubs struggling for the best position near their mother. The beast turned out to be a caring mom!

"Since you have followed me into my home", the bear spoke to the Princess, "you will have to stay here now. Soon it will be winter and these three little ones here need a lot of food to survive the long months of ice and snow."

"Will you then help me in return?", the Princess asked.

The bear only growled a deep roar and curled up on the floor.

The next morning the bear woke the Princess even before dawn and said:

"We need to go out to gather berries!"

The Princess quickly collected many berries. She carried them proudly in her dress that she used as a bag and deposited the pile in front of the bear on the ground.

"Do you want to poison my little ones?", mama bear grumbled angrily, because the Princess did not know which berries were edible and which were poisonous. She had collected them by their colours.

The next morning the bear woke the Princess again before dawn and said:

"We need to collect roots!"

All day long the Princess dug with her bare hands in the ground, until her hands bled, and she brought many roots back into the cave.

"Do you want to kill my little ones?", mama bear grumbled angrily again, because the Princess did not know which roots were soft and sweet and which were hard and indigestible. Once again, the beast pushed the entire heap out of the cave to leave it to the birds and mice.

The following morning the bear said to the Princess: "You do not know how to collect berries or roots. But catching mice should be easy to do. We have fed them for days now. Go out and catch mice."

The Princess went outside and tried her best. But she did not have the patience to wait long enough in front of a hole. She did not catch even one mouse. She returned at night empty handed.

"This way my little ones will not survive the winter!", the bear said greatly disappointed.

"I am so sorry that I cannot be of any help", the Princess replied with her head hung in shame. The bear only growled a deep roar and curled up on the floor.

The following morning, when the Princess awoke before daylight the bear was already out looking for food. The three little bears sat in the corner of the cave and looked at her with great anticipation.

"What will you bring us today?", they asked. "We are very hungry."

At this the Princess had a brilliant idea.

She went outside, broke a long branch off a bush, attached a thread that she pulled out of her torn dress and attached it to the rod. Then she collected worms and larvae she could use as bait. Equipped with this she went down to the river, looking for a spot on a rock just like the one that she knew from home. Many times, she had watched her husband catch fish, so she knew exactly how to do it. This time she returned to the cave with her apron full of fish. And this time the mother bear roared with satisfaction. After having given enough food to the little ones, she shared the remaining fish with the Princess. After the meal the Princess did not lie down to rest, but put herself to work to dry as many fish over a fire as she could.

The following days she continued doing the same, until the mother bear and her children grew big and fat. She now even had an extra supply of food for herself.

One day, all of a sudden, the bear did not leave the cave anymore and when the Princess stepped outside with her rod to catch more fish, she found the world white with snow. Even the river was covered with a layer of thick ice.

The Princes turned around and wanted to ask the bear. Surely now was the right time to finally give her the desperately needed advice she had so patiently been waiting for. But when she spoke to her, she did not even move. The bear slept so deep and sound that even shaking her would not make her open up one eye.

The Princess had no other choice but to go back to the castle of her parents. However, the snow was so deep that there was no trail to be seen anymore and she did not know in what direction to go. Besides, she did not have a coat to protect herself against freezing. Nothing else could be done but stay in the cave, surviving on dried berries and fish.

She was all alone in total silence. Not even the bear was there to speak to her. Some days it snowed so much that she could not even step outside to look at the sun, because the entrance was blocked with ice and snow.

Thus, many weeks passed with long nights of darkness and cold, as the Princess lived inside the cave of the bear. Until finally, one day, she heard the first bird singing happily. When she peeked outside, she noticed that early flowers had poked through the snow cover.

The bear and her cubs had become skinny during the winter weeks, so the Princess decided right away to go down to the river to catch new fish.

Standing on the rock in the strong current in the first warming beams of sunlight it happened that her husband came along the way on his horse. He also had waited for the winter to pass. He had gone abroad and had made his fortune in a foreign land, and now wanted to return home.

When he discovered a young girl standing on a rock, fishing like he himself had once done, he became very curious. The dress and the hair of the girl were so dirty and torn that he did not recognize his wife. But when he approached the maiden to speak to her, he noticed a big bear moving slowly close to her.

He calmly reached for his crossbow, moved slowly, so the bear would not hear him and soundlessly aimed at the animal.

The Princess discovered the hunter on the horse just in time. Immediately she understood the danger.

Without hesitation she threw away her rod, jumped in front of the bear spreading her arms to protect it. And because her fear for the bear's life was so great, she did not even recognize the familiar face of her own husband.

"Hold on, hunter! Do not do her any harm!", she yelled." There is no danger at all! Don't you see?"

The hunter and the girl looked at each other.

And at that very moment they recognized each other.

With great joy they ran towards one another, slung their arms in the air and hugged.

"Now you can go home", the bear spoke. "You do not need my advice any longer. The help you once wanted to force from me, you have found inside yourself. The winter is over. I have to move on and show the world to my little ones, so they will be able to survive on their own one day."

163

The Princess embraced the mother bear, handed over the last load of fish and climbed onto the horse behind her husband.

"Do not forget the cave", the bear said. "Whenever you are in need, you will find the answer there."

Then she turned around and trotted away.

The Princess and her husband happily returned to the castle. The joy and surprise about their return after such a long time was overwhelming.

On the same day of their return the royal couple passed a new law, proclaiming that from now on nobody was allowed to hunt for bears anymore.

And every spring time, the Princess went down to the river and left a basket full of fish there. And every year three bears with their cubs came to get them.

There was no need for the Princess to ever return to the cave, the Princess had found her true strength. And later on, she told the story to her children every night before bed time, and they passed it on to their children.

Märchenwelt der Transaktionsanalyse

Psychologische Märchen und Erzählungen für
Erwachsene zur Entwicklung der Persönlichkeit

ISBN: 978-3-7431-6319-5

Diese Sammlung neuer Märchen in traditionellem Stil ist für
alle Erwachsenen, die die Entwicklung der Persönlichkeit als
einen nie abgeschlossenen Prozess betrachten. Die
unterhaltenden Erzählungen basieren auf der Lehre der
Transaktionsanalyse (TA) und vermitteln eine Botschaft, die
der Leser auch ohne Kenntnisse der TA auf sich wirken lässt.
Jede Geschichte ist in sich abgeschlossen. Doch sie fügen sich zu
einem großen Gesamtbild zusammen, da sie in einem
Königreich spielen und die verschiedenen Figuren in den
Märchen immer wieder auftauchen. Die Erzählungen brechen
auf sanfte Weise mit traditionellen Rollenvorbildern, ohne die
Faszination der historischen Figuren zu verlieren

Mondo delle Favole Analisi Transazionale
Favole e racconti psicologici
per lo sviluppo della personalità
ISBN: 978-3749447145

Il Mondo delle favole nell'Analisi Transazionale è una collezione di favole per adulti interessati al tema dello sviluppo della personalità come un processo continuo. Esse sono narrate in uno stile antico simile alle favole storiche brevi. Operando a livello inconscio, ogni storia è creata sulla base della filosofia dell'Analisi Transazionale (AT), allo scopo di trasmettere messaggi impliciti che anche un lettore ignaro dei modelli e delle teorie dell'AT può apprezzare. I racconti sono raggruppati in storie singole, in cui non vi è una sequenza prescritta; tuttavia essi si congiungono a comporre una storia più grande le cui figure si rincontrano nello stesso regno. I racconti rompono delicatamente i ruoli e i modelli di comportamento tradizionale senza perdere il fascino delle figure storiche delle favole.